CRAVEABLE

SEEMA PANKHANIA

CRAVEABLE

ALL I WANT TO EAT

Photography by Haarala Hamilton
Illustrations by Evi-O.Studio

TEN SPEED PRESS
California | New York

For my mum,
the strongest woman in my life,
I owe everything to you

ALL I WANT TO EAT IS ...

5 SOMETHING COMFORTING [125]

6 SOMETHING SPECIAL [157]

7 SOMETHING SWEET [191]

8 SOMETHING NOW! [219]

WELCOME TO CRAVEABLE

Every day most of my thoughts are consumed with what I'm going to eat next. Literally every waking moment. If I'm not thinking about food, I'm asking my friends what they ate for breakfast, aimlessly strolling through supermarkets, or just scrolling through endless dishes on social media.

And since I think about food all day, when I'm hungry and need to cook, I've become very good at making dishes that specifically suit my cravings, which is kind of how this book was created.

I want this book to be a collection of simple (or simple enough!), trusted recipes that you can turn to to take some of the decision making out of your day – for when you need something spicy, salty, sweet, fresh, or just need to make a quick meal that's still delicious. It may be that it's super warm outside and you want something bright and fresh; perhaps you're bored at your desk and need something spicy to perk you up; or maybe you're just feeling like you need something cozy and comforting after a long, cold day.

As someone who usually shares their recipes on TikTok and Instagram, having them all written down in a book is so fantastic. Believe me, I know the hassle of watching something online, pausing and scrawling down notes to try and replicate it at home, and never quite knowing if you're doing it right. I also really love flicking through books for inspiration and knowing that they are more rigorously tested than a random recipe online, and hope this book can be that for you!

As much as I might like to be, I'm not a planner, especially when it comes to food. I understand and admire those who can meal prep, but the joy for me is creating something that just really fits what I need in that exact moment – I never really know what I'm going to eat in the evening on the morning of that same day, let alone the weekend before! It's just not how I cook. And though the world is always telling us that we should be meal prepping, batch cooking, and generally filling our fridges with as much food as possible, the 30 minutes that I spend at the end of each day making myself something delicious is as satisfying as it gets for me. Because of this, most of the recipes in this book use simple ingredients that you might already have at home or, if not, can easily be picked up from your local shop. Where slightly harder-to-find ingredients have been used, I have always tried to list a simple substitute that can be used without impacting the end result. There is also a full list of simple subs on pages 22–23.

Saying that, I don't want you to feel scared of using what you've already got in the pantry instead, or changing things up to make the recipes feel like your own. Be brave and adjust things to your taste and enjoy the journey along the way – just don't forget to taste as you go!

Above all, this book is yours and I hope that you turn to it time and again on those days when you just can't figure out what to cook. Fold the pages, write in the margins, spatter the recipes with sauce, and, most of all, enjoy!

Seema x

HOW I REALLY
GOT INTO COOKING

(AND SOME MORE BITS FOR ALL YOU NOSY PEOPLE OUT THERE)

As you can imagine, food has always been incredibly important to me – and if you ever had the chance to visit my mum's house, you would see exactly where that comes from! Food was the thing that always tied our family together. My mum made a fresh meal from scratch every single day: we never ate out, we never had takeout or frozen food, and we never ate in front of the TV. But at 7 pm every day, my family would gather around the dining table in our house in Slough. Prior to those mealtimes, my brother and I would often hover in the kitchen so that the rotli could come fresh out of the thava (cast-iron pan) and straight into our mouths. Usually, our meals were made up of some kind of curry, a dal, some pickles my mum had smuggled in her suitcase from India, papar (also known as poppadoms), and freshly made rotli with rice to follow. Looking back now, it really was a feast to be eating like this, especially when my mum was doing this every day while also juggling two jobs and two kids. I didn't appreciate it at the time, but I find it astonishing looking back at it now. She didn't have a big budget but somehow managed to create all of this absolutely delicious food, and I think that's something that's inspired me in my cooking, and hopefully something you'll see throughout the recipes in this book. Great food isn't about having hundreds of ingredients, it's about how you use the ingredients that you do have. In this way, my mum's cooking was what made me first fall in love with food, and so many of her dishes are still my go-tos when I want something

comforting. Making her Pea & Potato Curry (see page 146) or her 10-Minute Emergency Dal (see page 242) is what real comfort food cooking is for me.

My mum pretty much only made Indian food at home so that's what I ate every day growing up, but I was desperate to learn more about different foods from around the world. This took off in a major way when I ended up having to take a year off school after being diagnosed with cancer at age thirteen. It sounds much sadder than it was (or as I saw it at the time) – I wasn't really old enough to understand the severity of it all and, for me, it mainly meant that I got a lot of time off school to watch daytime TV, specifically the cooking channels! My mum made sure that I was able to fuel my newfound love by buying second-hand cooking equipment from garage sales and from eBay. (As a side note, I still get my cake pans from garage sales now and recommend you do the same – you can get great-quality, barely used pans for less than a dollar!) I ended up spending a year at home watching TV and baking to my heart's content, and by the time I was well enough to return to school, I was baking all my friends' birthday cakes (ones that looked like teddy bears and penguins) and even selling a few on Facebook!

I returned to school, now considering a career in food, but when it came down to picking my course of studies, a bit of research told me that culinary school

My older brother, Hitesh, and me.

would cost me over $50K upfront (which I obviously did not have), and getting a degree at a good college seemed like the more sensible choice. I studied at Manchester University, achieving a pretty good neuroscience degree, and throughout it all I cooked and learned as much as I could about food. Where I studied was next to a fantastically stocked East Asian supermarket, and though I had very little knowledge of East Asian food, I would trawl the aisles for new and exciting ingredients and bring them home to experiment, looking up recipes on YouTube and trying to replicate them myself.

On one of those nights I wanted to learn how to make a Filipino dish, since I had never tried any nor thought I would be able to visit the Philippines any time soon. Chicken adobo, the national dish of the Philippines, is chicken cooked with a cup of white vinegar and a cup of soy sauce. As you can imagine the entire dorm reeked of vinegar and my roommates, who were just about to leave for a night out, were fuming. But when the chicken simmered down, the vinegar tenderized the meat and the soy melded with the flavors and made it incredibly savory – it was one of the nicest meals I had ever made and none of us had ever heard of it before. I was so amazed at how simple it was and slightly angry that more people didn't know about it. I wanted to learn more dishes like this from around the world – simple, home-cooked dishes that anyone can make but are just a little less known – and that's how I started making every country's national dish.

As I was approaching graduation, I knew I didn't want a career in neuroscience or to be stuck in an office job in London. So I thought I'd give myself a year to try working in restaurants, and if, worst-case scenario, I hated it, I'd still be able to apply for grad school afterwards. I was already

sharing a few photos on my Instagram, and had gained a moderate following of just less than 2,000 (using the good ol' follow-and-unfollow technique) so I reached out to a few chefs that I admired to ask for advice. Only one (my favorite one) replied, Ravneet Gill. Rav invited me for a day to shadow her in the restaurant she was working at. Being an Indian girl who wanted to get into cooking, seeing any representation was close to nil, so seeing her succeed and have my dream job was so inspiring. Over the day she told me to forget all about culinary school (thank God! as where was I supposed to get over $50K from?!) and to get into a professional kitchen as soon as I could instead. So that's what I did.

The week I graduated from college I set up five trial shifts at different restaurants in London, leaving my top pick, Gordon Ramsay's Lucky Cat, for the final day. As the week went on, I got to know a bit about how restaurant kitchens work and what was expected of me, so on that final shift I was ready to make a stellar impression. I was offered a job the same day, and somehow was now a professional chef – it must've been the unwavering excitement of being in a kitchen that got me through.

The thing about working in restaurant kitchens is that the hours are horrendous. I was starting work at 8 am and would get home at 1 am; my mum would greet me at the door with a bucket of salted hot water to soak my legs and relax my muscles. Then she would give me a big glass of warm milk with honey and send me to bed, just so I could get up in the morning and do it again the next day. I did that for almost two years, every day riding my moped in from Slough to London.

It was exhausting, and although there were days when I almost couldn't bear to get on that moped and head off to work, I always did because I knew that working in the restaurant and learning all these new skills was going to open so many doors into a career I loved. Then one day the long hours caught up with me when I was riding to work in the rain, exhausted from a week of long shifts and probably not paying quite as much attention as I should have been. The car in front of me signaled right but I didn't notice and ended up crashing into the back of it as it turned a corner. I was actually pretty hurt and ended up being bundled into the back of an ambulance, but all I remember from that moment was the feeling of relief that I wasn't going to be able to go into the restaurant that day.

I took some time off to mend my fractured elbow and during that time MOB kitchen posted an application for an on-screen chef. By a strange stroke of luck, since I wasn't working 16-hour shifts, I was able to apply for the job, with the help of my brother and his girlfriend (now wife!). We created the most silly and ridiculous job application we could. I didn't end up getting that role, but I left the job in the kitchen and I started a side business selling brownies and doughnuts from my mum's house in Slough while I looked for work. The brownies were taking off. I spent weeks testing out recipes to get the perfect brownie and ended up shipping them all over the country. I'm very proud of that brownie recipe and you can find it on page 193.

During this stage, MOB called me up out of the blue, saying they remembered my silly video and wanted to offer me a role – as long as I was able to start the following Monday! Luckily (again!) I didn't have a job and so took them up on the offer immediately. I remember so vividly me and my brother squealing as soon as I got off the phone with Sophie Wyburd.

I had the best time working for MOB and loved being in that fun, creative environment with such talented people every day. I was able to spend my time learning about food and social media, and just really let my obsession for food take over – and all that with some of my favorite people I've met alongside me, it really was a dream job. It wasn't until Jake Gauntlett pushed me to make my own videos for the national dish series, which I had kept in my head since I first made that chicken adobo in college, that it all really took off. Soon I wanted to create more videos for my own page and have full creative freedom over them, so I took the leap and left MOB, but took all of the friendships I made there with me.

Now I get the privilege of being able to cook and create to my heart's content, trying out different styles of content, traveling to learn more about food, and keeping you all along on this journey with me. Whether you were one of those first 2,000 followers or if you're just joining me now, thank you so much for reading this far and for all the support you give. I really hope you enjoy this book. Social media can be a weird and scary place, but it can lead to some pretty special things.

WHAT ARE YOU CRAVING?

The way that I face the issue of what to eat for dinner usually just depends on what I'm craving in that exact moment. If it's a beautifully hot day then I'm most likely to want something fresh, but if I'm nursing a brutal hangover then I probably just need something (anything!) right now! So that's what I decided this book should be, a collection of recipes that suited every mood and craving. In doing so, I found that most of my moods and the cravings that matched them could be broken down into the following categories:

All I want to eat is something
_____fresh

All I want to eat is something
_____salty & savory

All I want to eat is something
_____spicy

All I want to eat is something
_____green

All I want to eat is something
_____comforting

All I want to eat is something
_____special

All I want to eat is something
_____sweet

All I want to eat is something
_____NOW!

And so that is how I have ordered this book. For the most part, the recipes are simple and can easily be made on a Tuesday night after work with perhaps just a quick trip to your local shop on the way home for the handful of ingredients that you don't already have on hand, though some are more labor-intensive. The Something Special chapter (pages 157–89) is for those times when you've got friends or family over and you want a project. For me, that time spent over the stove prepping a meal is itself a craving. I love those minutes and hours spent creating something fantastic that you know your guests will love. The Something NOW! chapter (pages 219–43) is the very opposite of that. These are my emergency recipes. They are generally meals for one, for when you're in a mad rush, perhaps feeling jaded and in need of an immediate pick-me-up that might otherwise come in the form of expensive takeout. I've put them at the back of the book, after even the desserts, so you have immediate access when the need arises.

My criteria for desserts is that they have to be showstopping and deliciously moreish, and I've created a whole chapter for you in this book. They are what turn occasions into something a bit more special. Just try and eat a Caramelized Banana Split (page 212) or take a bite of a Tangfastic Doughnut (page 194) and not have a smile on your face afterward.

I hope that ordering the recipes in this way makes as much sense to you as it does to me, but I'm also treating you to a slightly more traditional recipe list on the next page, just in case you do, in fact, simply want to find the dinner recipes.

17

A RECIPE LIST
(THE TRADITIONAL WAY)

SNACKS, STARTERS & SIDE DISHES

Beet & Feta Chaat	🍁 27
Cheese & Onion Borek	🍁 58
Crispy Chili-Garlic Roast Potatoes	🍁 141
Crispy Cumin Rice & Peas (Tahdig Style)	🍁 172
Crunchy Coconut & Sesame Broccolini	🍁 121
Egg-Fried Rice	🍁 175
Garlicky Anchovy Butter Smashed Potatoes	56
Glass-Shatteringly Crispy Kimchi & Potato Pancakes	🍁 55
Sambal Fish Sauce Wings with Cooling Green Onion Dip	81
Sticky Tamarind Cola Ribs	182
Sumac & Lime Oyster Mushrooms	🍁 110
Vinegary Mint Chutney	🍁 172

LIGHTER MEALS & SALADS

Bombay Fish Stick Sandwich	28
Caramelized Honey & Za'atar Grilled Cheese	🍁 70
Caramelized Red Onion & Zucchini Orzo Salad	🍁 117
Cheat's Doritos Chilaquiles	🍁 230
Crispy Ginger & Lime Bean Salad	🍁 41
Crispy Rice & "Seaweed" Salad	🍁 76
Emergency Dumpling Soup	🍁 221
Loaded Summer Rolls	🍁 44
Rotli	🍁 151
Secret Cheesy Masala Egg Muffin	🍁 62
Shrimp & Green Onion Pakora	66
Spicy & Sour Green Beans with Tuna	50
Tomato Caesar-esque Salad	42
Zingy Crispy Egg Cabbage Salad	🍁 34

VEGGIE MAINS

15-Minute Laksa	🍁 224
Bursting Cherry Tomato & Harissa Pasta	🍁 236
Cacio e Pepe Scissor-Cut Pasta	🍁 154
Cheat's Curried Omurice	🍁 130
Cheat's Leek & Brie Spanish Tortilla	🍁 73
Cheesy Gochujang Tortellini	🍁 233
Chili Paneer V8	🍁 91
Creamy Paprikash Beans	🍁 135
Curried Cabbage Wedges	🍁 162
Eggplant & Mushroom Iskender	🍁 106
French Onion Gnocchi	🍁 129
Icy Miso Noodle Soup	🍁 32
Jerk-Spiced Butter Cauliflower & Crunchy Maple Chickpeas	🍁 114
Keralan Egg Shakshuka	🍁 94
Miso Mushroom Carbonara-esque Spaghetti	🍁 138
Mum's Emergency 10-Minute Dal	🍁 242
Pea & Potato Curry	🍁 146
Peach & Halloumi Tacos	🍁 49
Pickled Jalapeño Mac & Cheese	🍁 144
Scotch Bonnet–Coconut Broth & Crispy Halloumi Noodles	🍁 98
Smoky Cauliflower & Pepper Shawarma Bowl	🍁 105
Smoky, Sticky Soy-Braised Tofu	🍁 65
Spicy, Garlicky Soy Sauce Pasta	🍁 228
Sticky Umami Mushroom Rice Bowl	🍁 118
Thai Basil Eggplant	🍁 122
Tomato & Peanut Udon	🍁 238
Za'atar Ricotta Dumplings	🍁 142

MEATY MAINS

SWEET DISHES

FIND YOUR OWN SPICE LEVEL

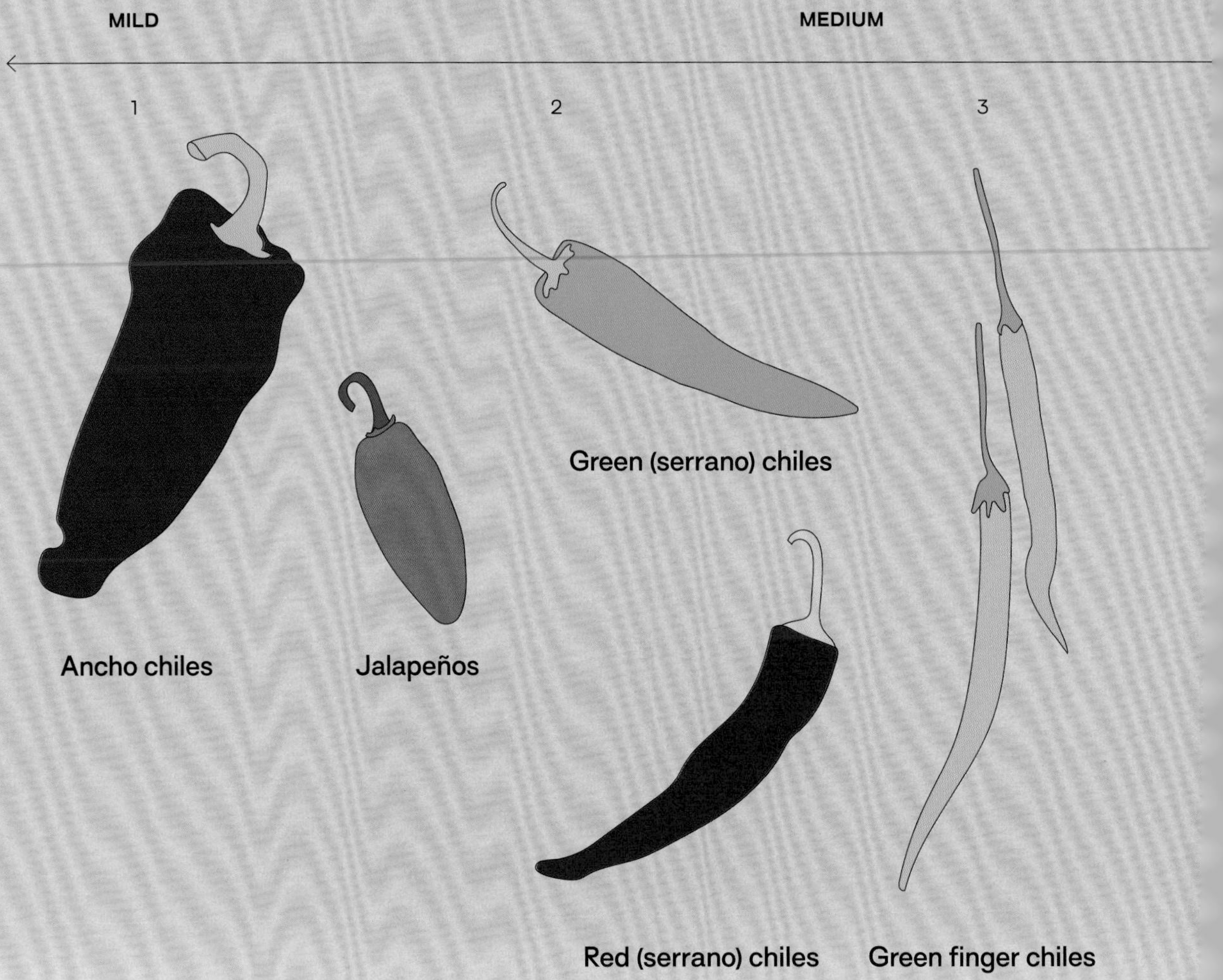

MILD

MEDIUM

1

2

3

Green (serrano) chiles

Ancho chiles

Jalapeños

Red (serrano) chiles

Green finger chiles

I've always thought that I had a pretty high tolerance for heat, a fact that I confidently repeated to a street food vendor on a trip to Thailand before being put firmly in my place as to what "spicy" actually was. Mouth burning and eyes watering, I had to come to terms with the fact that I do have a limit, and so do you. I like spicy food (there's a whole chapter in this book!) and the recipes that use chiles in this book do tend to pack a punch, but the beauty of making anything from scratch is that you can tailor it to your tastes. Feel free to reduce, omit, or even double-up on the chiles in these recipes. Find your own spice level. To help you get there, I've designed a table to give you a bit more info about the spice levels of the different chiles used in this book below. If you're eyeing a recipe with a Scotch bonnet and think you might find the heat too much, swap in whatever other chile you have on hand that better suits your spice preference.

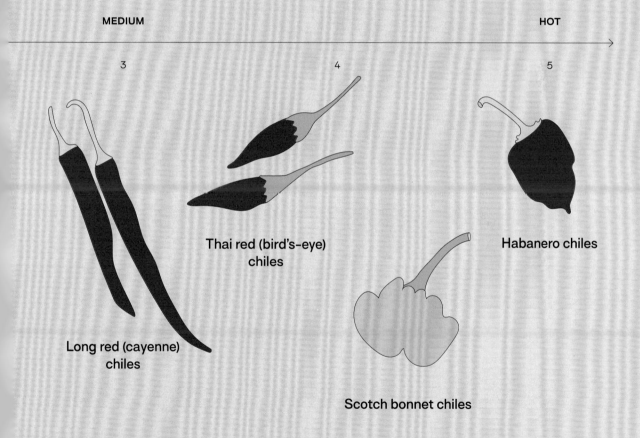

MEDIUM   HOT

3   4   5

Thai red (bird's-eye) chiles

Habanero chiles

Long red (cayenne) chiles

Scotch bonnet chiles

NOTE

→ Chiles store brilliantly in the freezer! I don't always get through fresh chiles fast enough so I store any extras in the freezer for whenever they are needed. No need to defrost, just use straight from frozen!

SIMPLE SUBSTITUTIONS

INGREDIENT		SUGGESTED SUBSTITUTIONS
Amchoor Powder	↔	Sumac or Lime Zest
Ancho Chiles	↔	Dried Chipotles or Guajillos
Anchovies	↔	Miso, Parmesan, or Chopped Bacon
Apple Cider Vinegar	↔	Sherry Vinegar or White Wine Vinegar
Bird's-Eye Chiles	↔	Long Red Chiles (Amount Halved)
Black Chinese Vinegar	↔	Balsamic Vinegar
Bombay Mix	↔	Any crunchy, spicy snack mix preferably with a mixture of noodles, pulses, and nuts
Chives	↔	Green Onions
Chorizo	↔	N'duja or Other Spicy Sausage
Coconut Oil	↔	Vegetable Oil
Coconut Yogurt	↔	Plain Yogurt
Coriander Seeds	↔	Cumin Seeds
Crème Fraîche	↔	Sour Cream or Yogurt
Dark Brown Sugar	↔	Light Brown Sugar
Dried Tarragon	↔	Dried Sage or Oregano
Dried Thyme	↔	Dried Rosemary
Fennel Seeds	↔	Cumin Seeds
Ghee	↔	Butter
Gherkins	↔	Pickles or Cornichons

I'm a firm believer in using the ingredients that you already have rather than having to spend precious time and money getting hold of special ingredients, and I want you to be the same when making the recipes from this book. If you come across an ingredient that you don't recognize or that you just can't be bothered to trek to the store for, give this list a scan and see if you can find it and its recommended substitute here. I've also listed these individually in the recipes themselves, but thought it would be useful to have them all in one place.

INGREDIENT		SUGGESTED SUBSTITUTIONS
Green Chiles	↔	Jalapeños
Green Lentils	↔	Red Split Lentils
Hoisin	↔	Honey
Nutritional Yeast	↔	Parmesan (or Any Hard Cheese), Grated
Parmesan	↔	Any Hard Cheese
Peanut Butter	↔	Any Nut Butter
Peanuts	↔	Cashews, Almonds, or Macadamia Nuts
Pretzels (Sweet Dishes)	↔	Graham Crackers
Radishes	↔	Celery
Red Onions	↔	White Onions
Rice Vinegar	↔	White Wine Vinegar or Apple Cider Vinegar
Shallots	↔	Onions (Amount Halved)
Shaoxing Rice Wine	↔	Dry Sherry, White Wine, or Mirin
Sour Cream	↔	Yogurt
Sriracha	↔	Any Other Hot Pepper Sauce
Sumac	↔	Combo of ½ Za'atar, ½ Sesame Seeds
Tahini	↔	Any Nut Butter
White Wine	↔	Chicken or Veg Stock (with a Splash of White Wine Vinegar)
Worcestershire Sauce	↔	Soy Sauce or Chopped Anchovies
Za'atar	↔	Combo of ½ Sumac, ½ Sesame Seeds

SOMETHING FRESH

BEET & FETA CHAAT

Chaat is one of the most underrated foods in India. It's an all-encompassing salad, fresh, sour, spicy, and crunchy. My mum would make this with yogurt, potatoes, and chickpeas, but in my version I've combined the sweetness of cooked beets with salty feta to achieve a parallel version. It's perfect with any curry or just on its own. Traditionally the crunch element would come from papri, which is fried dough, but I've used Bombay mix because it's a bit easier to find. However, if you find any crunchy fried puri in the Indian supermarket, give them a go!

8 oz / 225g cooked beets	
2 large tomatoes, cored	
1 x 14-oz / 400g can of chickpeas	
½ a red onion	
2 green finger chiles or red serrano chiles	
a small handful of fresh mint	
3 Tbsp tamarind paste	
2 Tbsp honey	↔ brown sugar or agave
½ tsp ground cumin	
¾ cup / 180g Greek yogurt	
3½ oz / 100g feta	
1 cup / 75g Bombay mix	↔ other crunchy, spicy snack mix
a small handful of pomegranate seeds	⌁ optional
salt	

Cut the beets into large chunks and the tomatoes into small pieces.

Drain and rinse the chickpeas.

Finely chop the onion, chiles, and mint.

Make the tamarind dressing by combining the tamarind paste with the honey, 2 Tbsp of water, and a pinch of the cumin. Season with salt.

In a bowl combine the beets, tomatoes, chickpeas, and onion and lightly season with salt. Spread the yogurt on your serving plate and top with the beet mixture.

Drizzle the tamarind dressing over the vegetables and crumble on the feta, then sprinkle with the chopped mint and chiles and the Bombay mix.

Finish with the pomegranate seeds, if using, and a sprinkling of the remaining cumin and enjoy.

COOK YOUR OWN BEETS

I love pre-cooked beets – all the fun without the mess. But if you want to use fresh, roast them at 400°F / 200°C, brushed with a little oil and wrapped in foil, for 45 to 60 minutes until tender. Allow to cool before using.

NOTES

→ *You could even drizzle over some green chutney (page 165).*

ALL I WANT IS SOMETHING ...

BOMBAY FISH STICK SANDWICH

Bird's Eye fish stick sandwiches are a cherished classic among British after-school snacks, to which Bombay mix adds the perfect crunchy coating without the hassle of deep-frying. This sandwich embodies the fusion of British convenience culture with the spice and crunch of Indian flavors. Nestled between slices of classic white bread – no sourdough here – and slathered with a curried tartar sauce, it's a fantastic choice for a fresh and satisfying lunch.

FOR THE BOMBAY FISH

2½ cups / 90g Bombay mix   ↔ other crunchy, spicy snack mix

8 oz / 225g white fish (cod is the classic choice)

2 Tbsp all-purpose flour

1 egg

FOR THE CURRIED TARTAR SAUCE

1 Tbsp finely chopped gherkins, plus more, sliced, for the sandwich   ↔ 1 large pickle or 6 cornichons

1 Tbsp capers, finely chopped

1 green chile, stemmed and finely chopped

2 Tbsp chopped fresh cilantro

1 clove of garlic, peeled

½ cup / 120g mayonnaise

1 Tbsp fresh lemon juice

1 Tbsp curry powder

salt and black pepper

FOR ASSEMBLY

4 thick slices of white bread

4 leaves of butter lettuce

¼ cup / 80g mango chutney   ↔ any other chutney

Preheat the oven to 375°F / 190°C.

Use a food processor to pulse the Bombay mix into large crumbs – you don't want a fine crumb.

Cut the fish into finger-length pieces.

Set up three bowls for a coating station: one with flour, one with a whisked egg, and one with the processed Bombay mix. Season the flour and egg bowls lightly with salt.

Coat each piece of fish in this order: flour, egg, and Bombay mix. Make sure to press the coating well onto the fish. Place the coated fish on a baking sheet and bake for 8 to 10 minutes, or until just cooked through.

While the fish is baking, combine the chopped gherkins, capers, chile, and cilantro in a bowl and grate in the garlic. Add the mayo, lemon juice, and curry powder, mix well, and season with salt and pepper.

Once the fish is done, assemble the sandwiches. Spread the curried tartar sauce on two slices of bread. To the other two slices add the lettuce, fish, chutney, and extra sliced gherkins. Sandwich it all together and enjoy.

NOTES

→ If you're looking for a shortcut, use store-bought tartar sauce.

→ You can freeze the coated fingers uncooked.

→ Experiment with various types of Bombay mix, such as Gujarati mix, chakri mix, or even balti mix.

AIR FRYER FRIENDLY

→ Pop the fish sticks into the air fryer using the same time and temperature.

ALL I WANT IS SOMETHING …

FRESH

ICY MISO NOODLE SOUP

This is for when it's scorching hot out or when you crave that fresh feeling from your lunch. Icy noodle soups are huge in Korea – I love them, and so will you. They are bright and pungent, and I've used cucumber water for another level of much-needed freshness – bonus points for getting in more liquid when it's so hot outside! This also takes inspiration from a cold Japanese soup called hiyajiru, which uses miso as the base. It's the same comforting feeling of having a hot soup on a cold winter day, but in reverse!

½ a cucumber

2 eggs

8 oz / 225g soba noodles

2 tsp tahini ↔ any nut butter

1¼ cup / 300ml water

2 Tbsp miso paste

1 tsp grated fresh ginger

1 tsp chili oil, plus more for serving

2 Tbsp apple cider vinegar ↔ sherry vinegar or white wine vinegar

a pinch of sugar

1 clove of garlic

4 green onions

2 cups / 300g crushed ice

salt

Smash the cucumber and roughly chop into small pieces. Place in a colander over a bowl, sprinkle with ½ tsp of salt, and let sit for 15 minutes to draw out the water.

Boil a big pan of water and boil your eggs for 6 minutes, simultaneously cooking the soba noodles in the same water according to the package instructions.

Rinse the noodles in cold water and set aside until ready to serve.

Peel the eggs and cut in half.

Whisk the tahini to a smooth paste with ¼ cup / 60ml of the water. Add the miso and whisk until smooth. Slowly add the remaining 1 cup / 240ml of water and the ginger.

Squeeze out the water from the cucumbers and add it to the miso broth along with any exuded liquid in the bowl. Taste for seasoning – depending on how salty your miso is, you may not need any more.

Combine the cucumbers in a bowl with the chili oil, vinegar, and sugar and grate in the garlic.

Thinly slice the green onions lengthwise and soak them in ice water to get them really crisp.

To serve, pile your soba noodles in the center of two bowls. Fill the outside with crushed ice. Top with the cucumber and egg, then pour the broth over the noodles.

Finish with more chili oil and the green onions and enjoy.

ALL I WANT IS SOMETHING …

NOTE
→ *Toast the miso by putting it on a baking sheet and broiling on the highest setting for 5 minutes. If you have a gas stove you can spread it over a metal spoon and gently brush it over the burner flame. It gives another layer of flavor to the miso paste!*

TIME	SERVES	VEGGIE (WITH SUBS)
20 MINUTES	2	

ZINGY CRISPY EGG CABBAGE SALAD

This salad is a burst of flavors and textures: crunchy cabbage, crispy eggs, and lots of veg. Salads are great for a quick lunch, and this one is inspired by spicy, zingy som tam, an incredibly spicy and sour papaya salad from Thailand, which I've drizzled with creamy peanut butter. Topped with an ultra-crispy fried egg, you can eat it in the middle of the day for lunch or as a side with a bigger meal later.

FOR THE DRESSING

2 cloves of garlic

1 to 2 Thai red chiles, stemmed   ↔ 1 to 2 long red chiles

6 Tbsp / 90ml fresh lime juice

¼ cup / 60ml fish sauce   ↔ veggie fish sauce

2 Tbsp light brown sugar

1 small head of cabbage, thinly sliced, about 1¼ lb / 600g (I used a mixture of green and red)

2 carrots, thinly sliced or grated

1¼ cups / 200g cherry tomatoes, halved

¼ cup / 65g smooth peanut butter   ↔ any nut butter

2 eggs

2 Tbsp peanuts, toasted and crushed

a small handful of fresh cilantro, roughly chopped

vegetable oil

salt

Smash the garlic and chiles with the back of a knife to form a paste – you don't want pieces of the chile in your sauce. Alternatively, you can blend the two together with the rest of the dressing ingredients.

In a bowl, combine the garlic, chiles, lime juice, fish sauce, and sugar.

Put all the veg into a large bowl and toss with the spicy dressing, reserving 1 Tbsp of the dressing.

Mix the peanut butter with ¼ cup / 60ml of warm water and the reserved dressing to make a sauce and add a pinch of salt.

Fry the eggs in oil until very crispy.

Plate up the cabbage salads. Drizzle with the peanut sauce and sprinkle with the crushed peanuts and chopped cilantro. Add the fried eggs on top.

NOTE
→   *To get the cabbage really thin, use a mandoline or a speed peeler, otherwise a sharp knife and a steady hand works great.*

TIME
45 MINUTES

SERVES
2

HAINANESE SALMON RICE

Hainanese chicken is one of my staple comfort foods. It's the national dish of Singapore, and don't tell the other countries, but it's my favorite of all the national dishes I've ever made. The chicken is poached in a ginger and green onion broth, which is then used to make the rice and served with a green onion oil and chili crisp. So incredibly simple but so delicious. This salmon version hits all the right spots, and you still get that crispy salmon skin that we all know and love.

¾ cup / 150g sushi rice   ↔ any short-grain rice

2 inches / 5cm ginger

5 green onions

1 cup / 240ml chicken stock

2 salmon fillets

1 Tbsp toasted sesame oil

chili crisp, for serving (see note)

soy sauce, for serving

2 Tbsp vegetable oil

salt

Wash the rice three times in cold water until it runs almost clear.

Cut 2 slices of the ginger and set the rest aside for later. Cut the whites off the green onions and roughly chop.

Put the rice into a pan with the chicken stock, sliced ginger, green onion whites, and ½ tsp of salt.

Bring the rice to a simmer. Place the salmon on top of the rice, skin-side up, decrease the heat to low, and put a lid on. Simmer for 10 minutes.

Meanwhile, finely chop the remaining green onions and ginger and place in a heatproof bowl. In a medium skillet, heat the vegetable oil to smoking point and pour over the green onions and ginger. Add a pinch of salt and set aside.

In the same medium skillet, heat the sesame oil until very hot. Remove the salmon from the rice, brushing off any rice pieces. Put the lid back on the rice and let it steam. Place the salmon skin-side down in the hot oil and cook for 1 minute, just to crisp up the skin.

Stir the rice well and taste for seasoning.

Serve the rice with the salmon, drizzled with the green onion oil, chili crisp, and soy sauce.

CHILI CRISP

Chili crisp is readily available in most supermarkets but if you want a speedy alternative, heat ¼ cup / 60ml of vegetable oil in a pan and add 3 cloves of garlic, 1 shallot, and 4 red chiles, all finely chopped. Cook over medium heat for 6 to 7 minutes until the oil is stained red. Transfer to a bowl and stir in ¼ tsp of salt and 1 Tbsp soy sauce.

NOTES

→ *Use any fish you like! You can also use chicken, but just make sure it's boneless so it cooks in the same time as the rice. My favorite is to use chicken thighs with the skin on, removing the bone (if necessary) and crisping up the skin just like the salmon at the end.*

→ *You can use store-bought chili crisp and skip the homemade one at left – that way you'll save 15 minutes and have it done in half an hour.*

ALL I WANT IS SOMETHING …

36

CRISPY GINGER & LIME BEAN SALAD

I've been trying to get into beans, and this salad has become my holy grail for meal prep lunches. Baking the beans makes them crispy and perfect for soaking up the sour lime dressing. It's served on a big pile of whipped cottage cheese for some added protein. So if you aren't sure about beans yet, this may just be the recipe to convert you!

1 x 14-oz / 400g can of chickpeas

1 x 14-oz / 400g can of butter beans or cannellini beans

1 x 14-oz / 400g can of red kidney beans

½ tsp ground cumin

1 Tbsp all-purpose flour

2 Tbsp nutritional yeast ↔ Parmesan or any hard cheese

2½ cups / 160g sugar snap peas, trimmed and halved lengthwise

2 celery stalks, thinly sliced

olive oil

FOR THE DRESSING

2 inches / 5cm ginger, grated

juice of 3 limes

¼ cup / 60ml extra-virgin olive oil

1 tsp miso paste ↔ 2 Tbsp soy sauce and 1 tsp tahini

1 tsp honey

½ tsp salt

½ tsp black pepper

TO SERVE

1 cup / 240g cottage cheese ↔ ricotta or thick yogurt

a large handful of fresh parsley, finely chopped

½ tsp salt

Preheat the oven to 375°F / 190°C.

Drain the chickpeas and beans and lightly rinse them. Put them into a bowl and toss with the cumin, flour, and nutritional yeast.

Spread the beans into a single layer on a baking sheet and drizzle with oil. Bake for 25 to 30 minutes, until the beans are crispy, tossing them halfway through. Let cool completely then transfer to a bowl.

Meanwhile, combine all the ingredients for the dressing.

Using a food processor, blend the cottage cheese, parsley, and salt.

Add the sugar snap peas and celery to the bowl of beans and toss with the dressing. Taste for seasoning.

Spread the cottage cheese on a plate and pile the crispy beans on top.

NOTE
→   This is a great way to use up any leftover beans you have in the back of the pantry – just throw in what you have!

ALL I WANT IS SOMETHING …

TOMATO CAESAR-ESQUE SALAD

Anything to do with Caesar salad is always fantastic. When tomatoes are bursting into season, this salty, savory dressing is perfect with them. I opted for no mayo in this dressing to keep it crisp and refreshing – think of it like panzanella meets Caesar salad! The tomatoes will soak up that savory dressing and add a burst of seasonal sweetness. And don't forget the whole anchovies on top for that delicious savory saltiness.

6 oz / 170g crusty stale bread	Preheat the oven to 375°F / 190°C.

6 oz / 170g crusty stale bread

4 oz / 115g thick-cut bacon,   ⌁ optional
cut into thick pieces

4 anchovies in oil, plus more for serving

juice of 1 lemon

1 tsp Dijon mustard

1 Tbsp Worcestershire sauce ↔ soy sauce

2 Tbsp red wine vinegar   ↔ apple cider vinegar or
white wine vinegar

2 cloves of garlic, grated

2 oz / 55g Parmesan, grated (about 1 cup), plus more
for serving

1 lb / 450g tomatoes

1 large handful of fresh basil

¼ cup / 60ml extra-virgin olive oil

salt

Preheat the oven to 375°F / 190°C.

Tear the bread into large chunks. Add to a baking sheet with the bacon, if using, drizzle with the oil from the anchovy jar, and bake in the oven for 15 minutes until golden and crisp.

Finely chop the anchovies, mashing them with a knife to form a paste. Put them into a bowl and whisk in the lemon juice, mustard, Worcestershire sauce, and vinegar. Add the garlic and Parmesan. Finally, whisk in the oil.

Chop the tomatoes into large chunks and toss them in a bowl with a large pinch of salt. Let them sit for 5 minutes, then add the dressing. Once the croutons have cooled, add them to the bowl and mix together very well so that the bread can absorb the dressing.

Throw in the fresh basil leaves last of all, then top with additional whole anchovies, add a sprinkling of Parmesan, and enjoy immediately.

NOTES

→   Skip the whole anchovies if you aren't a fan, but keep the ones in the dressing and mash them up well – they add such a great savoriness that can't be missed!

→   Using seasonal tomatoes is what is really going to make them shine, especially if you can find the beautiful heirloom ones! If you are going to splurge on anything for this dish, make it the tomatoes.

AIR FRYER FRIENDLY

→   Crisp up the croutons and bacon in the air fryer using the same time and temperature as you would with the oven, checking after 5 minutes and shaking regularly.

LOADED SUMMER ROLLS

Vietnamese summer rolls are always my go-to fresh food when I feel like I need lots of delicious vegetables all wrapped up in a little bundle. They are great to take with you on the go, and fantastic for using up bits in the fridge. I've combined these summer rolls with an equally delicious Malaysian roll called popiah. Popiah have sauce slathered on the inside and are packed to the brim with crunchy onions and nuts, which is exactly what I want in my summer rolls.

8 oz / 225g vermicelli rice noodles

8 oz / 225g portobello mushrooms, cut into ½-inch / 1.3cm slices

¼ tsp sugar

1 clove of garlic, grated

1 cup / 100g bean sprouts

5 eggs

8 rice paper rounds

⅓ cup / 95g hoisin sauce

⅓ cup / 80g sriracha

a small handful of fresh cilantro, roughly chopped

1 head of baby gem lettuce, shredded

½ cucumber, cut into thin batons

¼ cup / 30g roasted salted peanuts, roughly chopped

3 Tbsp crispy shallots or onions

vegetable oil

salt

FOR THE DIPPING SAUCE

¼ cup / 60ml fish sauce   ↔ veggie fish sauce

2 cloves of garlic, finely chopped

1 red chile, stemmed and finely chopped

3 Tbsp hot water

1 tsp sugar

juice of 1 lime

Place the vermicelli noodles in a heatproof bowl. Pour boiling water over them and let them soak for 3 to 4 minutes (check the package instructions), then drain and rinse in cold water.

Put the mushrooms into a dry nonstick skillet with a big pinch of salt and cook for 5 minutes over high heat to draw out the moisture. Once the mushrooms are browned, add 1 Tbsp of oil, the sugar, and garlic. Cook for 2 minutes, until the mushrooms are crisp, then transfer to a plate and set aside.

Heat the empty pan with a small glug of oil and fry the bean sprouts for 30 seconds with a pinch of salt until just softened, then transfer to a plate and set aside.

Whisk the eggs in a bowl and add to the same pan (no need to wash it). Cook on each side for 2 minutes to make a thin omelet. Roll up the omelet and cut it into ½-inch / 1.3cm slices.

Pour some cold water onto a plate, checking it fits your rice paper rounds. Soak one of the rounds for no more than 30 seconds, making sure all of it touches the water. Place it on your cutting board – don't worry if it's not totally soft yet as it will soften as you add the fillings.

Brush 2 tsp each of hoisin and sriracha over the moistened rice paper then add the mushrooms, omelet strips, cilantro, lettuce, bean sprouts, rice noodles, cucumber, peanuts, and crispy shallots.

Roll it up like a burrito, folding in the sides. Repeat with the rest of the rice paper rounds and filling.

For the dipping sauce, combine all the ingredients in a small bowl, mixing well so the sugar dissolves.

Serve the summer rolls with the dipping sauce.

> **PEANUT DIPPING SAUCE**
> If you are vegetarian or would just prefer a peanut dipping sauce, whisk together 3 Tbsp of peanut butter with 1 Tbsp of hoisin, 1 Tbsp of soy sauce, 1 Tbsp of sriracha, and 3 Tbsp of hot water.

FRESH

ALL I WANT IS SOMETHING . . .

PEACH & HALLOUMI TACOS

The sweet, honeyed flavor of peaches and the salty, crispy halloumi make these tacos brim with fresh flavors in no time. I've called for peaches here as they are more accessible, but when you can get hold of perfectly ripe figs – and unfortunately this is only for a precious few weeks a year – you need to make sure to stock up and indulge as much as you can.

If you can get your hands on some hot honey, that would be perfect here!

3 peaches, pitted and quartered ↔ 6 figs

½ a red onion, finely chopped

2 green chiles, stemmed and finely chopped

1 Tbsp olive oil, plus more to cook the halloumi

⅓ cup / 100g sour cream ↔ yogurt

1 green onion

a small handful of fresh cilantro, finely chopped

juice of 1 lime

8 oz / 225g halloumi

½ tsp red pepper flakes

¼ cup / 85g honey

8 to 10 corn tortillas

hot sauce (I like El Yucateco or Cholula), for serving

salt and black pepper

Combine the peaches, onion, half of the chopped chiles, and the oil in a bowl and season with salt and pepper.

Blitz up the sour cream, remaining chile, green onion, cilantro, and lime juice. Season with salt and pepper.

Cut the halloumi into small pieces and cook in a hot pan with a drizzle of oil until golden and crispy.

Combine the red pepper flakes and honey in a microwave-safe jar and microwave for 30 seconds to 1 minute or until bubbling.

Heat up the tortillas and layer the green sauce, peaches, and halloumi on top. Finally, drizzle with the honey and hot sauce, if you like, and enjoy.

HOT HONEY

If you love hot honey, empty a jar of honey into a saucepan with a few teaspoons of red pepper flakes and heat until bubbling. Let cool then decant back into the honey jar and use as normal.

AIR FRYER FRIENDLY

→ *If you prefer, cook the halloumi in the air fryer for a few minutes until crisp and golden.*

ALL I WANT IS SOMETHING …

SPICY & SOUR GREEN BEANS WITH TUNA

This recipe came about when I'd come back from a long weekend away, eating out and drinking, and just needed something nourishing but still special. It ended up being a mix of a tuna niçoise and a som tam. It's very sour and spicy, which ties all the veg together perfectly and makes you feel so good after.

8 oz / 225g baby potatoes, halved

2 eggs

2 oz / 55g green beans, trimmed

1 head of baby gem lettuce, leaves torn

1 shallot, thinly sliced

½ a cucumber, sliced

⅔ cup / 110g cherry tomatoes, halved

1 x 5-oz / 140g can of tuna, drained

salt

FOR THE DRESSING

2 to 3 Thai red chiles, stemmed and finely chopped/pounded   ↔ 2 tsp spicy chili oil

3 Tbsp fish sauce

juice of 2 limes

1 tsp sugar

2 cloves of garlic, grated

salt

TO SERVE

a small handful of peanuts, crushed

fresh cilantro

chili oil

Bring a large pot of salted water to a boil, then add the potatoes and boil for 15 minutes. In the final 6 minutes add the eggs, and in the final 4 minutes add the green beans. Drain.

Peel the eggs and cut in half.

Combine the ingredients for the dressing and season with salt.

Toss the potatoes, green beans, lettuce, shallots, cucumber, and tomatoes in a bowl with most of the dressing.

Transfer to a serving bowl and top with the tuna, eggs, and the remaining dressing.

Sprinkle with the peanuts, cilantro, and chili oil, if needed.

NOTE

→ *For milder heat, use long red chiles. If you can pound the Thai red chiles and garlic in a mortar and pestle, you won't get big pieces of chile in your salad! You can also soak the sliced shallots in ice water so they are not as pungent.*

ALL I WANT IS SOMETHING …

ALL I WANT IS …

SOMETHING SALTY & SAVORY

GLASS-SHATTERINGLY CRISPY KIMCHI & POTATO PANCAKES

Korean kimchi pancakes are to die for, but I wanted them glass-crackingly crispy. I make these in a similar way to latkes, the fantastically crisp Jewish potato fritters, which makes them incredibly crispy, with a sour and a little spicy kick from the kimchi. And the Parmesan crust just makes them even more delicious and more crunchy.

12 oz / 340g russet potatoes, peeled and grated

¾ cup / 170g kimchi, drained and finely chopped

2 Tbsp all-purpose flour

1 Tbsp cornstarch

1 egg

1 Tbsp gochujang

½ tsp sugar

½ tsp salt, plus more for the crème fraiche

2 oz / 55g Parmesan cheese, grated (about 1 cup)   ↪ veggie Parmesan or any hard cheese

⅔ cup / 160g crème fraîche   ↪ sour cream

1 Tbsp toasted sesame oil

1 Tbsp honey

vegetable oil

Combine the potatoes and kimchi and squeeze out as much liquid as possible with your hands or inside a clean kitchen towel.

Put the squeezed veg into a bowl and add the flour, cornstarch, egg, gochujang, sugar, and salt. Mix well.

Heat ½ inch / 1.3cm of vegetable oil in a nonstick skillet over medium heat and when it's hot add a few 1-Tbsp dollops of the batter, flattening them out into thin circles. Fry for 3 minutes on each side, then transfer to a wire rack to drain. Repeat with the remaining batter.

Pile the Parmesan directly in the pan in heaps a similar size to the pancakes. Add the pancakes on top and allow the Parmesan to crisp up. Place back on the wire rack to cool and crisp up further.

In a bowl combine the crème fraîche, sesame oil, honey, and a pinch of salt.

Serve the crispy fritters with a dollop of the crème fraîche and enjoy.

NOTES

→   When buying kimchi, ingredients such as fish sauce or shrimp paste guarantee an umami boost, but look for versions without if you're veggie! And try looking for jars with an earlier expiration date, meaning they have been fermenting longer and will be more zingy! A good kimchi is zingy, crunchy, and a little spicy.

→   If you aren't a fan of kimchi, try sauerkraut.

→   Starchy potatoes such as russets are best for these, but in a pinch any white potato will work!

ALL I WANT IS SOMETHING…

SALTY & SAVORY

GARLICKY ANCHOVY BUTTER SMASHED POTATOES

Anchovies are a new love affair of mine, and now I can't get enough of them. They bring the perfect blend of saltiness and brininess, and a punch of flavor to any dish. Here I've taken the little fishes, mashed them up with some butter, and generously spread this umami goodness all over crispy potatoes. All balanced by the dreamy sour cream dip – perfect for that salty craving.

1 lb / 450g baby potatoes

6 Tbsp / 85g unsalted butter

4 cloves of garlic, grated

10 anchovies, finely chopped, plus more for serving

¼ cup / 60ml vegetable oil

FOR THE SOUR CREAM DIP

a large handful of fresh chives, finely chopped ↔ green onions, finely chopped

1 Tbsp onion powder

juice of ½ a lemon

1 cup / 240g sour cream

salt and black pepper

Put the potatoes into a pot of lightly salted cold water. Bring to a boil, then reduce the heat to a simmer and cook for about 15 minutes, or until the potatoes are fork-tender.

Meanwhile, preheat the oven to 450°F / 230°C.

In a saucepan, melt the butter and add the garlic and anchovies. Cook this mixture for about 5 minutes, or until the butter starts to brown, then turn off the heat.

Set aside 1 Tbsp of chives for garnish, then put the rest into a bowl and combine with the onion powder, lemon juice, and sour cream. Season with salt and pepper.

Once the potatoes are cooked, drain them and transfer them to a baking sheet. Using the bottom of a measuring cup or something similar, gently smash each potato, being careful to keep them mostly intact.

Drizzle the smashed potatoes with the oil, lightly sprinkle them with salt, and roast them in the oven for 20 to 25 minutes, turning them halfway through. Once the potatoes are nice and crispy, brush them generously with the anchovy butter.

To serve, spread the sour cream dip on a plate, place the crispy potatoes on top, and finish with more anchovy butter and anchovies and a sprinkling of the reserved chives.

NOTES
→   If you're on a trip to Italy or Portugal, stockpile anchovies and bring them back in your hand luggage.

→   If you're not quite sold on anchovies (though I urge you to give them a try because they're delightful), you can try swapping them for a tablespoon of miso, a handful of Parmesan, or a few chopped slices of cooked bacon!

AIR FRYER FRIENDLY
→   Bake the potatoes in the air fryer using the same time and temperature you would the oven.

ALL I WANT IS SOMETHING . . .

CHEESE & ONION BOREK

Cheese and onion pasties, or hand pies, are iconic. They are the perfect train snack, and it was my go-to Greggs pasty flavor whenever we ventured out of my hometown of Slough and into the depths of London. I've used this filling inside Turkish börek, an incredibly crispy filo-wrapped pastry – so you get the gooey cheese and onion flavor we all know and love, inside a glass-shattering shell.

3 large onions, roughly chopped

10 Tbsp / 140g unsalted butter

3 cloves of garlic, chopped

1 lb / 450g potatoes, peeled and cut into chunks

7 oz / 200g sharp   ↤ your favorite cheese
Cheddar, grated (a scant
2 cups)

1 tsp chopped fresh thyme

½ tsp black pepper

6 Tbsp / 90ml heavy cream

8 sheets filo pastry (about 8 oz / 225g)

1 tsp nigella seeds   ↤ sesame seeds
                     ⁓ optional

salt

Preheat the oven to 375°F / 190°C and line a baking sheet with parchment paper.

Put the onions into a large pot with 2 Tbsp of the butter and a pinch of salt. Cook over medium heat for 20 to 25 minutes until golden and caramelized. Add the garlic and cook for another 3 minutes.

Meanwhile, put your potatoes into a large pan of water and bring to a boil. Boil for 15 minutes, or until fork-tender, then drain.

Set aside a handful of cheese to top the pies before they bake.

Put the potatoes into a large bowl. Add the caramelized onions, thyme, pepper, ½ tsp of salt, cream, and remaining cheese. Mash together and taste for seasoning.

Melt the remaining 8 Tbsp / 110g of butter in a small pan. Lay one sheet of filo on the work surface and brush liberally with the melted butter. Add another layer of filo and brush again.

Spoon a quarter of the potato mixture along the longest edge and roll up the filo, encasing the potato filling to make a tube. Then roll again to make a spiral shape, pressing it in tightly. Place on your baking sheet, brush with some more butter, and sprinkle with the reserved cheese and some nigella seeds, if using.

Repeat with the remaining filo and filling (you may not need all the butter).

Bake in the oven for 20 minutes or until very crispy.

Let cool slightly and serve warm or at room temperature.

AIR FRYER FRIENDLY
→ *Bake the borek in the air fryer using the same time and temperature.*

ALL I WANT IS SOMETHING …

SECRET CHEESY MASALA EGG MUFFIN

Eggs in Gujarat are a fantastic nighttime food staple – take note of the importance of nighttime. Because Gujarat is largely vegetarian and eggs are considered meat, many women don't approve of their husbands eating them, so the men sneak out at night to go in secret to satisfy their cravings, and boy, they are delicious. I think the secrecy makes them that much more spectacular. You get almost every variety of egg, smothered in spices. My favorite was the masala scrambled egg, which I've placed inside a traditional English muffin, with crunchy bacon and quick curried ketchup.

½ a red onion, finely chopped

1 green chile (finger chile), stemmed and finely chopped

¼ of a red or yellow bell pepper, finely chopped

1 clove of garlic, grated

½ tsp grated fresh ginger

½ tsp chili powder

1 tsp garam masala

4 strips bacon ⁓ optional

2 English muffins

4 eggs

2 oz / 55g Cheddar cheese

5 cherry tomatoes, quartered

1 Tbsp unsalted butter

2 slices of American cheese

3 Tbsp ketchup

vegetable oil

salt and black pepper

In a nonstick skillet, add a glug of oil and gently fry the onion, chile, bell pepper, garlic, ginger, chili powder, and ½ tsp of the garam masala for 5 minutes over low heat until the spices are bubbling and the vegetables have softened.

Remove from the heat and transfer to a bowl. Let the pan cool completely.

If using, fry the bacon to your liking in another skillet (or in the oven), then heat up the muffins in the bacon grease or warm in a toaster.

Crack the eggs into the bowl of vegetables, then grate in the Cheddar and add the tomatoes. Gently mix together so that the spices are evenly distributed and add ¼ tsp of salt and some black pepper.

Add the butter to the cooled pan and pour in the egg mixture. Turn the heat to the lowest setting and cook the eggs, using a spatula and folding to create very soft scrambled eggs.

Portion into two rounds in the pan and add a slice of American cheese to the top of each one. Pop a lid on top for 30 seconds and allow the cheese to melt.

Mix together the ketchup and remaining ½ tsp of garam masala. Add half of the spiced ketchup to the bottom half of each muffin, then add a portion of cheesy eggs, 2 slices of bacon, if using, and the top of the muffin.

NOTE

→ *Try the eggs in between two soft pieces of white bread.*

ALL I WANT IS SOMETHING …

SMOKY, STICKY SOY-BRAISED TOFU

Smoked tofu is a hidden gem in the supermarket. It infuses a delightful smokiness throughout a dish, creating an incredible depth of flavor. I've concocted a spicy-sweet sauce to drench the tofu, and it all comes together in under 30 minutes. (And guess what? It's air fryer friendly!)

8 oz / 225g block of firm smoked tofu, sliced into thin squares

5 cloves of garlic

1½ inches / 4cm ginger

1 tsp five-spice powder

3 Tbsp hoisin sauce   ↔ honey

¼ cup / 60ml soy sauce

1 Tbsp Shaoxing rice wine   ↔ dry sherry, white wine, or mirin

½ tsp red pepper flakes

2 star anise

4 cloves

1 cinnamon stick

1 onion, cut into large chunks

vegetable oil

Pan-fry the tofu slices in a little oil for 2 minutes per side or until they turn golden.

Grate the garlic and ginger into a liquid measuring cup and add the five-spice powder, hoisin, soy sauce, rice wine, red pepper flakes, and the whole spices.

Heat a wok over high heat, add a little oil, then add the onion and fry for about 3 minutes until softened. Add the sauce mixture along with ⅔ cup / 160ml of water and bring to a boil. Add the tofu and cook for 5 minutes until the sauce thickens and coats the tofu.

Serve the tofu over a bowl of hot rice and enjoy!

NOTES

→   If you don't have whole spices don't fret – use ¼ tsp of ground, or simply omit them.

→   And if you can't find smoked tofu, regular firm tofu will work, but you'll miss out on that delectable smoky flavor.

AIR FRYER FRIENDLY

→   For an equally delicious result, pop the tofu into the air fryer at 400°F / 200°C for 10 to 15 minutes until it turns golden.

ALL I WANT IS SOMETHING …

SHRIMP & GREEN ONION PAKORA

An iconic British Chinese takeout staple, shrimp toast, combined with my favorite Indian snack, bhajia (or pakora as you might call them). The fried bread makes these extra crispy, with pockets of juicy shrimp for all the things you love in a shrimp toast. My tip is to add spinach for some crunch and a few tablespoons of Parmesan for an extra savoriness – don't worry, it won't taste cheesy! Dunk these in some sweet chili sauce for a banging snack.

12 oz / 340g raw medium shrimp, peeled and deveined, tails on

4 oz / 115g crusty stale white bread

1 bunch of green onions, roughly chopped

2 cloves of garlic, minced

1 tsp minced fresh ginger

¼ cup / 35g sesame seeds, plus more for sprinkling

2 Tbsp grated Parmesan

1 tsp light soy sauce

¼ tsp white pepper

½ tsp salt

½ cup / 70g all-purpose flour

1 tsp baking powder

a large handful of baby spinach

sweet chili sauce, for serving

vegetable oil, for deep-frying

Reserve 4 oz / 115g of the whole shrimp, then tail and roughly chop the remaining 8 oz / 225g, leaving a mix of large and small pieces for texture. Tear the bread into chunks similar to the chopped shrimp.

Put the chopped shrimp, green onions, garlic, ginger, sesame seeds, Parmesan, soy sauce, white pepper, and salt into a bowl. Mix well, then add the flour, bread, baking powder, 5 Tbsp / 75ml of water, and the spinach. Mix with your hands.

Add enough oil to a Dutch oven or deep skillet to deep-fry and heat to 350°F / 175°C. Gently, using your hands (this creates the best crunchy texture, rather than spoons), form 3 Tbsp of batter into a round in your hand, top with a tail-on shrimp, and sprinkle with sesame seeds.

Fry a few together at the same time for 5 to 6 minutes until golden brown and crispy. Drain on paper towels and repeat with the remaining batter, shrimp, and sesame seeds. Enjoy with sweet chili sauce.

ALL I WANT IS SOMETHING . . .

CARAMELIZED HONEY
& ZA'ATAR GRILLED CHEESE

I love the combination of salty and sweet – honey and cheese are my go-to fridge snacks when I need a quick bite. Toasting the outside of the bread with caramelized honey gives a slightly nutty but very chewy texture that makes this grilled cheese to die for.

1 oz / 30g aged Cheddar cheese

1 oz / 30g Gruyère cheese   ↔ Comte
or more Cheddar

2 Tbsp unsalted butter, softened

2 slices of sourdough bread   ↔ crusty white bread

2 Tbsp honey

2 tsp za'atar, plus more for sprinkling

pickled chiles, for serving

sea salt flakes

Grate both cheeses and combine in a bowl.

Spread the butter liberally on both sides of the bread and stuff the grated cheese and 1 tsp za'atar between them, reserving about 1 Tbsp of cheese.

Place a skillet over low heat and add the sandwich. Cook very gently for 10 minutes, flipping halfway through, until the cheese is bubbling and hot and the outside is golden and crisp. Add a splash of water and put the lid on to help the cheese melt.

Sprinkle half the reserved cheese directly into the pan and put the sandwich on top – the cheese will melt and caramelize onto the bread. Repeat on the other side.

Take the sandwich out of the pan and turn the heat off. Drizzle the honey and 1 tsp za'atar into the hot pan and allow them to bubble. Put the sandwich back into the pan and swirl it around in the honey.

Remove from the pan and sprinkle with more za'atar and flaky sea salt.

Cut the sandwich into pieces and enjoy hot, preferably with pickled chiles.

NOTE
→   Use whatever combination of cheeses you like. And play around with different spice mixes such as 1 tsp ras el hanout or even Old Bay seasoning if you don't have any za'atar.

ALL I WANT IS SOMETHING …

CHEAT'S LEEK & BRIE SPANISH TORTILLA

If you've been reading through this book you know I love a good hack, or anything to save me some time or hassle in the kitchen. I always seem to have oven fries in the freezer, and this makes perfect use of them, coating them with caramelized leeks and Brie cheese to make a gooey Spanish tortilla.

1¼ lb / 570g frozen thick-cut oven fries (skinless)

¼ cup / 60ml extra-virgin olive oil, plus more for cooking tortilla

1 large leek, white part only, cleaned and thinly sliced

6 cloves of garlic, thinly sliced

6 eggs

7 oz / 200g Brie cheese

salt

Preheat the oven to 400°F / 200°C. Place the fries on a baking sheet, drizzle with 2 Tbsp of the oil, and bake for 15 minutes.

Add the leeks and garlic to a skillet with the remaining 2 Tbsp of oil. Cook these down over medium heat for 20 minutes with a big pinch of salt until very soft and caramelized.

Crack all the eggs into a large bowl and very gently mix together – you don't want them completely combined. Add the leeks, garlic, and fries and let sit for 10 minutes.

Meanwhile, cut the cheese into thick slices.

Pour a small glug of oil into a 10-inch / 25cm nonstick skillet and pour in half the egg mixture.

Layer on the sliced Brie and top with the remaining egg mixture.

Put a lid on the pan and cook over medium-low heat for 15 minutes until the cheese is very melty but the top of the eggs is still soft.

Flip over onto a plate and slide the tortilla back into the pan. Cook for 30 seconds more and then flip onto a plate and enjoy while hot.

NOTES

→   Switch out the Brie with any gooey cheese you like, maybe Taleggio, Fontina, or even Reblochon if you're feeling fancy.

→   You can also use this as a base for any flavor of Spanish tortilla – add some chorizo, some caramelized onions . . . you would be surprised how many things go well with potatoes and eggs.

ALL I WANT IS SOMETHING . . .

CHORIZO & PEA POZOLE

One of my favorite soups in Mexico was pozole. The base is surprisingly light, but it's topped with lots of hearty vegetables and crunchy bits, making it full of textures and flavors, so every bite is different from the last. Traditionally it's made with hominy, which is produced from dried corn, but I've used peas in mine, roasted to get that nutty, sweet flavor. The chorizo gives an extra depth of flavor, similar to Mexican dried chiles!

4 cups / 520g frozen peas

1 lb / 450g chorizo   ↔ spicy sausage

1 tsp cumin seeds

1 Tbsp chipotle paste, or use one chipotle chile from a can in adobo

1 large tomato, roughly chopped

½ an onion, roughly chopped

6 cloves of garlic, roughly chopped

2 qt / 1.9L chicken stock

olive oil

salt and black pepper

FOR THE TOPPINGS

¼ head of green cabbage, shredded

5 radishes, diced   ↔ celery

a small handful of fresh cilantro, finely chopped

3 cups / about 100g tortilla chips

1 tsp dried oregano

2 limes, halved

Preheat the oven to 400°F / 200°C.

Pour half of the peas onto a baking sheet, drizzle with oil, and sprinkle with salt. Roast for 20 minutes, or until very crispy, stirring halfway through.

Remove the casing from the chorizo. Slice half of it and crumble the rest with your hands. Add to a dry skillet with the cumin seeds and cook for 10 minutes over medium heat to render the fat.

Meanwhile, blitz the chipotle paste, tomato, onion, and garlic with ¾ cup / 175ml of chicken stock in a food processor, until smooth.

Add the blended tomato mixture and remaining chicken stock to the skillet with 1 tsp of salt and some pepper, then bring to a simmer and cook for 15 minutes.

Add the uncooked peas to the skillet and cook for 2 minutes.

Divide the soup between four bowls and top with the crunchy peas, shredded cabbage, radishes, cilantro, and a handful of tortilla chips. Sprinkle with oregano, squeeze the juice of half a lime into each bowl, and enjoy.

CRISPY RICE & "SEAWEED" SALAD

One of my all-time favorite dishes was at Chet's in London, where I first tried the wonders of the very spicy crispy rice salad, also known as nam khao tod. It's a fantastic combination of crispy rice pockets and fresh herbs, and a classic Chinese takeout hack of making kale taste like seaweed! I've been using it as my go-to method for using up leftover rice, and I love it so much that I sometimes make extra rice just to have leftovers for this salad.

1 bunch (about 7 oz / 200g) curly kale, stems removed, leaves torn into small pieces

1½ tsp plus 2 Tbsp sugar

1 tsp MSG

6 cloves of garlic

4 to 6 Thai red chiles, stemmed

2 inches / 5cm ginger, roughly chopped

about 3½ cups / 500g cold cooked rice

2 Tbsp cornstarch

1 shallot, thinly sliced

3 Tbsp fish sauce   ↔ veggie fish sauce

3 Tbsp fresh lime juice

a small handful each of fresh mint + cilantro, chopped

1 celery stalk, sliced

a small handful of peanuts, toasted and chopped

2 heads of baby gem lettuce

vegetable oil

salt

NOTES

→ If you don't have any day-old rice, you can cook 1¼ cups / 250g of rice as usual. Spread the hot rice on a baking sheet and let it cool, then dust it with cornstarch and you're ready to continue with the recipe.

→ You can also make the rice crispy in the oven or air fryer. Just drizzle a baking sheet with oil, spread out the rice, and bake at 400°F / 200°C for about 30 minutes, giving it a good stir every 10 minutes until very golden and crisp.

→ I've left the type of rice unspecified as it truly doesn't matter. I've prepared this salad with various types of rice and it always turns out fantastic.

Preheat the oven to 425°F / 220°C.

Toss the kale with 2 Tbsp of oil, ½ tsp of salt, 1 tsp of the sugar, and the MSG. Spread out on a baking sheet and roast in the oven for 5 minutes until very crispy.

Pound the garlic, all but one of the chiles, and ginger together in a mortar and pestle. Add 3 Tbsp of oil, 1 tsp of salt, and ½ tsp of the sugar. Mix well. Alternatively, you can blend it all with an immersion blender.

Place the mixture in a microwave-safe bowl and microwave on high for 2 minutes until it starts sizzling.

Combine the cooked rice with the cornstarch. Toss it well with your hands, then add the microwaved oil mixture and mix well.

Heat a cast-iron skillet over high heat. Add a generous amount of oil – enough to cover the bottom of the pan. Add the rice in a thin layer and press it down firmly. Decrease the heat to medium and cook for 10 minutes without stirring, until the rice at the bottom of the pan has become very crispy and golden.

Carefully flip the rice disk using a spatula. If it breaks apart, don't worry. Cook on the other side for 5 minutes until it's golden, then remove it from the pan and let it drain on paper towels to remove excess oil. Break it into shards.

While the rice is cooking, soak the shallots in ice water.

Finely slice the reserved chile. Make the dressing by combining the fish sauce, remaining 2 Tbsp of sugar, the lime juice, the sliced chile, and 3 Tbsp of warm water. Mix well to dissolve the sugar.

Drain the shallots and toss with the rice, herbs, celery, and crispy kale. Dress with the fish sauce dressing and top with the toasted peanuts. Separate the baby gem leaves and use them to scoop up the rice.

SOMETHING SPICY

SAMBAL FISH SAUCE WINGS WITH COOLING GREEN ONION DIP

Sambal is one of my favorite ingredients to keep on hand; it's a Malaysian-style chili paste that can be made in hundreds of different ways, and when you find your perfect version you won't be able to get enough of it. Smother it on chicken wings, with lots of fish sauce to add a zinginess and freshness for the perfect bite. I've even dunked the wings in a cooling garlicky green onion sauce – it's an homage to Frank's buffalo wings with a blue cheese sauce!

2½ lb / 1.1kg chicken wings

4 long red chiles, stemmed

½ tsp red pepper flakes

8 cloves of garlic, peeled

1¼ inches / 3cm ginger

1 lemongrass stalk   ⌁ optional

3 shallots, peeled

1 Tbsp tomato paste

¼ cup / 50g sugar

¼ cup / 60ml fish sauce

juice of 2 limes

3 Tbsp unsalted butter

¼ cup / 60ml vegetable oil

salt

FOR THE GARLIC AND GREEN ONION SAUCE

5 green onions, finely chopped

3 cloves of garlic, grated

⅓ cup / 80g mayonnaise

⅓ cup / 80g sour cream

1 Tbsp fresh lime juice

salt and black pepper

Preheat the oven to 425°F / 220°C.

Pat the wings dry with paper towels and liberally salt on all sides. Place them on a baking sheet and bake for 20 minutes, then turn and bake for another 10 minutes until golden and crispy.

Meanwhile, blitz up the chiles, red pepper flakes, garlic, and ginger in a food processor, adding 2 Tbsp of water to help it blend.

Heat up the vegetable oil in a heavy pan over medium heat. Add the chile mixture and cook for 10 minutes until the oil is stained red.

Bash the lemongrass with the back of a knife so the fibers come loose, then roughly chop. Blend the shallots and lemongrass together in the food processor.

Add the blended shallots and lemongrass to the chile mixture along with the tomato paste, and cook for 10 minutes over medium heat until thickened and dark red.

Whisk in the sugar, fish sauce, lime juice, and butter. Taste for salt – it may not need more depending on how salty the fish sauce is.

Mix together all the ingredients for the garlic and green onion sauce and season with ½ tsp each of salt and black pepper.

Once the wings are cooked, place them in a bowl and pour in the chile sauce. Toss well so they are evenly coated.

Serve with the garlic and green onion sauce and enjoy.

NOTES

→   You can easily double my sambal recipe and keep it in the fridge for up to a month.

→   Use ¼ cup of a store-bought sambal for a really quick version!

ALL I WANT IS SOMETHING …

SINGAPORE CHILE SHRIMP BURGERS

One of my favorite things that I ate in Singapore was chile crab, a cultural icon. A sweet and tomatoey sauce, enriched with eggs and used to smother giant crabs. We also got a black pepper butter crab which was so buttery and peppery. We ended up combining the two crabs and it created the most delicious bite we could have imagined – peppery, spicy, and slightly sweet. I've encompassed that glorious bite into a burger.

   To make it more budget friendly I've opted for shrimp instead of crab, but feel free to switch out the shrimp for 8 oz / 225g lump crab meat, or even any cooked fish for an easy fish patty.

FOR THE SHRIMP PATTIES

8 oz / 225g medium raw shrimp, peeled and deveined, tails removed

2 green onions, finely chopped

1 egg white

½ tsp white pepper

2 Tbsp soy sauce

¼ tsp salt

¾ cup / 90g fine breadcrumbs

FOR THE SAUCE

½ an onion, roughly chopped

4 cloves of garlic, roughly chopped

½ inch / 1.3cm ginger, grated

3 long red chiles, stemmed and roughly chopped

½ tsp chili powder

1 tsp black peppercorns, crushed

¼ cup / 65g ketchup

1 Tbsp soy sauce

vegetable oil

TO SERVE

4 green onions, thinly sliced

juice of 1 lime

2 burger buns

¼ cup / 60g mayonnaise

1 tsp toasted sesame oil

½ a clove of garlic

butter lettuce

Very finely chop half of the shrimp (or blitz them in a food processor) and roughly chop the rest. Put them into a bowl with the green onions, egg white, white pepper, soy sauce, salt, and half of the breadcrumbs.

   Divide the mixture in half and shape into patties. They'll be a bit sticky, so press them into the remaining breadcrumbs to coat evenly. Chill the patties on a plate in the fridge while you make the sauce.

   Put the onion, garlic, ginger, and chiles into a bowl with a splash of water and use an immersion blender to blitz them into a smooth paste (you can also finely chop them).

   Heat a generous glug of oil in a saucepan and sauté the onion mixture for 5 minutes. Add the chili powder, black peppercorns, ketchup, soy sauce, and 6 Tbsp / 90ml of water. Cook for 2 minutes, mix well, and once combined, turn off the heat. Taste and season with salt.

   Heat about 1½ inches / 4cm of oil in a skillet and gently shallow-fry the shrimp patties for 5 minutes or until golden on all sides. Once they are cooked, transfer them to a plate lined with paper towels to absorb any excess oil, then return the pan to the heat and toast the burger buns until golden.

   Combine the 4 green onions with a pinch of salt and the lime juice.

   Combine the mayo and sesame oil and grate in the garlic.

   Now to assemble the burgers: spread the mayo generously on the bottom halves of the buns. Add a few leaves of lettuce, the patties, and then the spicy sauce and zesty green onions. Finish with the top halves of the buns and enjoy!

NOTE

→   *Don't let any leftover sauce go to waste! It's fantastic for sandwiches or drizzled over some rice with a fried egg.*

SPICY

ALL I WANT IS SOMETHING . . .

CRISPY CHILE CUMIN LAMB

If your Chinese takeout order is the classic crispy shredded beef, you are going to love his spicier, punchier girlfriend: crispy, juicy lamb in a sticky coating of chile and cumin sauce. Pile it on top of a mountain of egg-fried rice for an easy weeknight classic.

SPICY

1 lb / 450g boneless lamb shoulder or leg

1 tsp baking soda

1 egg white

½ cup / 70g cornstarch

1 large onion

2 red chiles, stemmed

4 green onions

1¼ inches / 3cm of ginger

4 cloves of garlic

1 Tbsp cumin seeds

10 dried Sichuan chiles ⁓ optional

vegetable oil

salt

FOR THE SAUCE

2 Tbsp Chinese black vinegar ↔ balsamic vinegar

¼ cup / 60ml soy sauce

1 Tbsp dark soy sauce

½ tsp white pepper

2 to 3 Tbsp chili crisp (see note, page 36)

1 to 2 tsp red pepper flakes

1 tsp cornstarch

Slice the lamb into thin strips against the grain. Put it in a bowl with the baking soda, massage well, and marinate for 30 minutes in the fridge. (This is called velveting and makes the meat more tender.) Rinse off the baking soda and pat dry. Then put the lamb into a bowl with the egg white, cornstarch, and a pinch of salt.

Meanwhile, cut the onion into large chunks, thinly slice the red chiles, and chop the green onions into 1½-inch / 4cm pieces. Grate the ginger and roughly chop the garlic.

Combine the vinegar, soy sauce, dark soy, white pepper, chili crisp, and red pepper flakes with 3 Tbsp of water.

In a large wok heat 1¼ inches / 3cm of oil (enough to shallow-fry the lamb). Carefully add the lamb in a single layer and cook for 3 minutes until it is crispy and cooked through. You can do this in two batches if necessary. Drain on paper towels.

Pour off all but 2 Tbsp of oil from the wok. Add the cumin seeds, onion, ginger, garlic, green onions, and red chiles. (Add the whole dried Sichuan chiles now, if using.) Fry over high heat for 4 minutes until charred and crispy. Add the lamb and sauce, along with a slurry made with the cornstarch and 6 Tbsp / 90ml of water.

Allow the sauce to bubble and coat the lamb. Serve immediately.

NOTE
→ Freezing the lamb for 30 minutes before slicing will help you cut it thinner. Substitute with beef, chicken, or even seitan!

ALL I WANT IS SOMETHING …

SPICY

FIERY SCOTCH BONNET LENTILS WITH CRISPY SALMON

My national dish series has been one of the biggest inspirations for my recipes, and this is a take on Nigeria's iconic jollof rice. It's an incredibly spicy tomato-based rice flavored with the mighty Scotch bonnet chile. These tiny yet fiery peppers pack not only intense heat but also remarkable depth and even hints of floral notes. I've transformed lentils into a rich and spicy sauce reminiscent of jollof rice and crowned them with crispy, succulent salmon to balance the heat, finishing with a drizzle of fresh green onion oil.

FOR THE LENTILS

1 large onion, finely chopped

2 large beefsteak tomatoes (about 1 lb / 450g), cored

2 inches / 5cm ginger, grated

6 cloves of garlic, chopped

1 Scotch bonnet chile, stemmed

1 red bell pepper, stemmed, seeded, and chopped

½ tsp allspice   ⎯ optional

3 Tbsp tomato paste

1 cup / 200g green lentils   ↔ red split lentils

1 tsp salt

olive oil

FOR THE GREEN ONION OIL

¼ cup / 60ml vegetable oil

4 green onions, finely chopped

2 inches / 5cm ginger, finely chopped

salt

FOR THE SALMON

4 skin-on salmon fillets   ↔ any other fish or protein

1 tsp curry powder

1 tsp salt

vegetable oil

Sauté the onion in plenty of oil for 5 minutes until golden.

Meanwhile, blend the tomatoes, ginger, garlic, Scotch bonnet, bell pepper, and allspice, if using, using an immersion blender until smooth.

Add the tomato paste to the sautéed onion and cook for 5 minutes until it darkens. Add the blended tomato mixture, cook for 5 more minutes until it bubbles, then add the lentils, salt, and 2 cups / 475ml of water. Cook over medium heat for 30 minutes until the lentils are tender, adding more water if needed.

Meanwhile, to make the green onion oil, heat the vegetable oil in a small saucepan until sizzling. Add the green onions and ginger to a heatproof bowl and carefully pour in the hot oil. Mix and season with a pinch of salt.

Rub the salmon all over with the curry powder and salt. Heat a skillet over high heat and add a generous amount of oil. Let it heat up, then add the salmon and cook skin-side down for 3 minutes. Flip and cook for 2 more minutes until the salmon is tender and cooked through.

To serve, place the hot lentils on plates, top with the crispy salmon, and drizzle with the green onion oil.

NOTES

→ *To get perfectly crispy salmon skin without sticking, cook the salmon skin-side down on a piece of parchment paper in the pan. Super crispy skin and no sticking!*

→ *Cut the cooking time in half by using pre-cooked green lentils or red split lentils. Use half the tomato sauce ingredients, add the cooked lentils, and simmer for 10 minutes.*

→ *You can leave the salmon out entirely and serve the spicy lentils with rice as a comforting dal.*

ALL I WANT IS SOMETHING …

PEANUTTY SALSA MACHA NOODLES

There are endless variations of chili crisp all over the world, and one of my favorites is Mexican salsa macha. With smoky dried chiles, nuts, seeds, and an abundance of garlic, this is really something special. Here I've combined it with one of my favorites, Chinese dan dan noodles, using its spicy, nutty sauce with ground meat, to make this incredibly moreish bowl.

FOR THE SALSA MACHA

½ cup / 120ml vegetable oil

6 cloves of garlic, roughly chopped

3 ancho chiles, stemmed   ↔ see notes
and seeded

3 Tbsp peanuts   ↔ cashews, almonds,
or macadamia nuts

1 Tbsp chili powder

3 Tbsp sesame seeds

FOR THE ANCHO SAUCE

1 ancho chile, stemmed   ↔ see notes
and seeded

2 cloves of garlic, peeled

2 Tbsp soy sauce

1 Tbsp oyster sauce

1 Tbsp tomato paste

1 lb / 450g ground pork   ↔ any ground protein

½ tsp salt

1 tsp cornstarch

vegetable oil

TO SERVE

1 lb / 450g round wheat   ↔ other wheat noodles
noodles or udon noodles

4 Tbsp / 65g peanut butter   ↔ any nut butter

4 Tbsp / 60ml soy sauce

4 tsp dark soy sauce   ⟿ optional

2 limes, halved

4 green onions, thinly sliced

First make the salsa macha. Heat the oil in a saucepan. Add the garlic, anchos, peanuts, chili powder, and sesame seeds and cook over medium-low heat for 10 minutes until the garlic is golden.

Transfer to a heatproof bowl and let cool slightly, then blend in a food processor to form a chunky salsa.

To make the ancho sauce, bring ½ cup / 120ml of water to a boil in a saucepan. Add the ancho, garlic, soy sauce, oyster sauce, and tomato paste. Boil for 5 minutes, then blend in the food processor.

Mix the pork and salt with the cornstarch. Place a pan over high heat, add a glug of oil and the pork, and cook until crispy, 6 to 8 minutes. Add the blended ancho sauce and cook for 5 minutes until thick and sticky.

Meanwhile, cook the noodles according to the package instructions and drain, reserving the cooking water.

Divide the peanut butter, soy sauce, and dark soy, if using, among four serving bowls. To each bowl add 1 to 2 Tbsp of salsa macha, the juice of half a lime, and 2 Tbsp of reserved cooking water (from the noodles) and top with the noodles, pork, and green onions. Enjoy!

NOTES
→   If you find a store-bought salsa macha you can use it to make these noodles in no time! You can also use ground chicken or any other ground meat here too.

→   This recipe makes more of the salsa macha than you will need, but it will keep really well in a sealed jar in the fridge for up to a month and is delicious drizzled over breakfast eggs, added to a lunchtime grilled cheese, or for zhuzhing up a salad.

→   If you can't find whole ancho chiles, substitute dried chipotles or guajillos – you can play around with whatever Mexican chiles you find, but just check how spicy they are! If you use red pepper flakes, substitute 1 tsp of flakes for 1 whole chile.

SPICY

ALL I WANT IS SOMETHING …

CHILI PANEER V8

This Indo-Chinese classic is ordered every single time I enter an Indian restaurant. It's the perfect mix of Indian and Chinese food, and my family have very strong opinions about how it should be made. This has been in the works for the past five years and it's the best version yet – even my mum said so!

SPICY

FOR THE PANEER

2 Tbsp all-purpose flour

2 Tbsp cornstarch

1 tsp chili powder

½ tsp salt

12 oz / 340g paneer, cut into cubes

1 Tbsp vegetable oil, plus more for frying

FOR THE SAUCE

2 large red onions, 1 finely chopped, 1 cut into chunks

1½ inches / 4cm ginger, finely chopped

7 cloves of garlic, finely chopped

4 to 6 green finger chiles,   ↤ jalapeños
stemmed and
finely chopped

1 tsp chili powder

1 tsp cumin seeds

¼ cup / 60ml soy sauce

2 Tbsp ketchup

2 Tbsp sriracha   ↤ your fave hot pepper
                              sauce

½ tsp sugar

1 Tbsp unseasoned rice vinegar

1 green bell pepper, stemmed, seeded, and cut
into chunks

½ tsp five-spice powder   ⁓ optional

½ tsp salt

½ tsp white pepper

2 green onions, finely chopped

Combine the flour, cornstarch, chili powder, and salt in a small bowl.

Toss the paneer with 1 Tbsp of oil in a medium bowl, then add the flour mixture and toss to coat. Freeze the paneer for 30 minutes.

Pour enough oil to shallow-fry the paneer into a large wok. Heat the oil to 350°F / 175°C, then add the paneer in a single layer and fry for 2 to 3 minutes until golden and crisp on all sides. Transfer the paneer to paper towels to drain.

Wipe out the wok with paper towels, then add a couple of glugs of fresh oil and return the wok to the heat. Add the onions, ginger, garlic, chiles, chili powder, and cumin seeds to the wok and cook for 5 minutes until softened.

Meanwhile, combine the soy sauce, ketchup, sriracha, sugar, and vinegar with ¾ cup / 175ml of water. Add to the wok and bring to a simmer.

Add the paneer, bell pepper, five-spice, salt, and white pepper. Toss well and allow to heat through for 4 to 5 minutes, adding a splash more water if necessary to get your preferred thickness of sauce.

Taste for seasoning, then sprinkle with the green onions and serve on its own or with rice.

NOTE

→ *Freezing the paneer makes it extra soft inside, but skip this step if you don't have time.*

ALL I WANT IS SOMETHING …

KERALAN EGG SHAKSHUKA

Keralan egg curry is a fantastically simple South Indian curry of hard-boiled eggs simmered in a spicy coconut sauce. The sauce itself is enriched by the sweetness of caramelized onions, along with coconut milk to mellow out the fiery heat. I've taken that sauce and used it as the base for this shakshuka, making it perfect with a soft, jammy egg and crusty bread on lazy weekends.

Try serving this with rice for a jammy egg curry!

SPICY

3 Tbsp unrefined coconut oil ↔ vegetable oil

2 large onions, thinly sliced

½ tsp fennel seeds ↔ cumin seeds

3 green chiles, stemmed and roughly chopped

4 cloves of garlic, roughly chopped

1¼ inches / 3cm ginger, roughly chopped

1 x 14-oz / 400g can of crushed tomatoes

1 tsp chili powder

1 tsp garam masala, plus more for sprinkling

¾ cup / 175ml canned coconut milk

3 to 4 eggs

salt

TO SERVE

crusty bread

1 lime, halved

Melt the coconut oil in a heavy pan. Add the onions, fennel seeds, and a big pinch of salt. Cook for 15 to 20 minutes until the onions are caramelized and jammy.

Meanwhile, pound together the chiles, garlic, and ginger in a mortar and pestle – alternatively, grate or finely chop them.

Add the chile-garlic mixture to the pan and cook for 5 minutes until fragrant. Add the tomatoes and spices and cook for another 20 minutes until the sauce is very thick. Add the coconut milk and bring to a simmer.

Make some wells in the sauce and crack the eggs into the holes. Put a lid on the pan and allow it to very gently bubble for 6 to 7 minutes until the whites are set but the yolks are still a bit runny.

Serve with crusty bread, a squeeze of lime, and a final sprinkling of garam masala over the top.

ALL I WANT IS SOMETHING…

SMASHED KEBAB BURGERS

In our household, the closest we came to a Sunday roast was our regular dinners at Taste of Pakistan in Hounslow where we would indulge in their incredible chapli kebabs. These kebabs are known for being thin, juicy, and perfectly spiced – which made me wonder how I haven't already put them in a burger. It took a bit of trial and error to get the correct flavors without compromising the crispiness – just make sure you press down hard! They're filled with charred peppers for that "mixed grill" feel, and topped with melty cheese for the ultimate lamb burger.

FOR THE GARLIC BUTTER

3 Tbsp unsalted butter, softened

3 cloves of garlic, grated

1 Tbsp chopped fresh cilantro

¼ tsp salt

4 burger buns

1 large onion, finely sliced

1 green bell pepper, stemmed, seeded, and finely sliced

2 tsp cumin seeds

1¾ lb / 800g ground lamb

4 green chiles, stemmed and finely chopped

1 clove of garlic, grated

½ tsp grated fresh ginger

1 tsp chili powder

1 tsp coriander seeds

1 tsp black pepper

8 slices American cheese

1 large tomato, thinly sliced

vegetable oil

sea salt

FOR THE CHILE-CILANTRO MAYO

a large handful of fresh cilantro, finely chopped

3 green chiles, stemmed and finely chopped

juice of 1 lemon

½ cup / 120g mayonnaise

To make the garlic butter, mix the butter, garlic, cilantro, and salt in a bowl. Spread the garlic butter over the cut sides of the buns.

Put the onion and bell pepper into a bowl with 1 tsp of the cumin seeds and ¼ tsp of salt.

To make the burgers, combine the lamb, chiles, garlic, ginger, chili powder, coriander seeds, the remaining 1 tsp of cumin seeds, and the black pepper in a bowl. Mix very gently and divide into eight balls.

Cut out two 4-inch / 10cm squares of parchment paper (you can reuse them!).

Get your largest cast-iron pan hot and toast the buttered burger buns until golden. Then drizzle the pan with oil and heat until smoking hot. Find a flat-bottomed pan that will fit inside the cast-iron one.

Place one lamb ball in the cast-iron pan, sprinkle generously with salt, then place a square of parchment on top and smash down as hard as you can using the second pan. Repeat with the other lamb balls and remove the parchment. Cook for 2 minutes – when you see moisture on the top of the lamb, scrape the bottom with a metal spatula and flip.

Cook for another 2 minutes. Add a slice of cheese to each patty and cover with a lid for 1 minute to allow the cheese to melt. Repeat with the other patties then transfer the burgers to a baking sheet and keep warm.

Add the onion and pepper mixture to the hot pan and cook over high heat for 5 minutes until caramelized.

To make the mayo, whisk the cilantro, chiles, lemon juice, and a pinch of salt into the mayonnaise.

Spread the mayo on the bottom halves of the buns. Layer on a few tomato slices and then the burger patties (two per bun) and top with the pepper mixture. Finish with the top halves of the buns.

SCOTCH BONNET–COCONUT BROTH & CRISPY HALLOUMI NOODLES

SPICY

Scotch bonnet peppers are among my favorite chiles to use, as they bring an abundance of flavor without the need for many other ingredients. These peppers are incredibly spicy, with a slightly floral aroma, making them perfect for soups. When paired with creamy coconut milk they create a delicious and warming broth that tastes like it's been cooking for hours.

1 red onion, roughly chopped

3 inches / 7.5cm ginger, roughly chopped

6 cloves of garlic, roughly chopped

1 tsp curry powder

1 Scotch bonnet chile, stemmed and roughly chopped

2 Tbsp tomato paste

1 x 14-oz / 400ml can coconut milk

¼ cup / 35g all-purpose flour

2 eggs, beaten

2½ cups / 200g unsweetened shredded coconut ↔ breadcrumbs

1 lb / 450g halloumi, cut into small cubes

1 lb / 450g instant ramen noodles

8 oz / 225g baby bok choy, halved

a small handful of fresh cilantro, finely chopped

2 limes, halved

vegetable oil

salt

Blend the onion, ginger, garlic, curry powder, and Scotch bonnet in a food processor to create a chunky paste.

Heat some oil in a skillet and sauté the onion paste for 10 minutes until fragrant. Stir in the tomato paste and cook for another 5 minutes until it darkens in color.

Add the coconut milk and 2 cups / 475ml of water and bring to a gentle simmer.

Prepare three bowls: one with the flour, one with the beaten eggs, and one with the shredded coconut. Season each bowl with a pinch of salt.

Heat enough oil in a saucepan for shallow-frying. Dredge the pieces of halloumi in the flour, then egg, then coat them with coconut. Fry the halloumi pieces until they are golden brown and crispy, about 3 minutes per side.

Cook the noodles in boiling water according to the package instructions. Cook the bok choy in the same water for 3 minutes.

Place some cooked noodles in each serving bowl, pour in the coconut broth, and top with the crispy halloumi, bok choy, and a sprinkling of chopped cilantro. Squeeze lime juice over each bowl and serve.

ALL I WANT IS SOMETHING …

NOTE

→　You can substitute the halloumi with crispy chicken, or tofu (and swap the eggs with oat milk) for a vegan-friendly version.

AIR FRYER FRIENDLY

→　Coat the halloumi with a spritz of oil and air fry at 375°F / 190°C for 10 to 15 minutes until it turns crispy and golden.

KOREAN-ISH FRIED POPCORN CHICKEN

This iconic sticky and spicy sauce is inspired by one that was developed in the trenches of my first (and last) food truck event with MOB Kitchen where people lined up for over two hours just for a taste of a Korean fried chicken burger. I've taken the same sauce, developed it some more, and slathered it on crispy fried chicken for the perfect bite. I opted for sour cream here instead of the conventional mayo because when mayo gets heated it can split, but this sauce stays luscious, with a tang to cut through the fattiness of the chicken.

FOR THE CHICKEN

1 lb / 450g skinless, boneless chicken thighs

¾ cup / 180g sour cream   ↔ yogurt

1 tsp gochujang

1 tsp apple cider vinegar

1 egg, beaten

1 cup / 140g cornstarch

1 cup / 140g all-purpose flour

enough vegetable oil for deep-frying

salt

FOR THE SPICY SAUCE

5 green onions, finely chopped

1¼ inches / 3cm ginger, grated

3 cloves of garlic, grated

¾ cup / 180g sour cream

6 Tbsp / 90g gochujang

2 Tbsp soy sauce

2 Tbsp chili crisp (we used Lee Kum Kee)

1 Tbsp apple cider vinegar

1 Tbsp honey

Cut the chicken into bite-size pieces and put them into a bowl with the sour cream, gochujang, vinegar, and egg. If you like you can let it marinate for 30 minutes or up to overnight to tenderize the chicken.

For the spicy sauce, mix the green onions, ginger, and garlic with the sour cream, gochujang, soy sauce, chili crisp, vinegar, and honey.

Pour enough oil into a pan to deep-fry the chicken and heat to around 350°F / 175°C.

Combine the cornstarch and flour in a bowl and season generously with salt. One by one, coat the chicken pieces in the flour mixture, scrunching them with your hands to make them craggy – this will make the chicken extra crunchy.

Deep-fry the chicken in batches for 4 to 5 minutes until golden brown, crispy, and cooked all the way through – cut a piece in half to check.

Toss the fried chicken in the spicy sauce and serve hot.

NOTES

→   *Feel free to use chicken breast for something leaner, but it is less forgiving when frying so it can dry out. You could even make this with tofu!*

→   *I used sour cream for the chicken marinade instead of yogurt for tenderization, so you don't have to deal with half a tub of sour cream in the fridge (since it's in the spicy sauce as well), but you can use a combination, or just yogurt if that's what you have!*

ALL I WANT IS SOMETHING …

ALL I WANT IS ...

SOMETHING GREEN

SMOKY CAULIFLOWER & PEPPER SHAWARMA BOWL

When I'm craving a lot of vegetables, roasting them with loads of spices makes a really simple but super-satisfying dinner. This is my take on the iconic shawarma bowl from the halal guy's cart in New York, covered with sauces but also lots of vibrant veg. It's all about balance, eh?

4 white pitas

4 Tbsp olive oil

2½ tsp smoked paprika

1 head of cauliflower, chopped into florets

1 red bell pepper, stemmed, seeded, and sliced

1 x 14-oz / 400g can of chickpeas, drained

3 cloves of garlic

2 tsp ground cumin

2 Tbsp dried oregano

salt

1¾ cups / 350g basmati rice

½ tsp ground turmeric

FOR THE SAUCE

½ cup / 120g thick Greek yogurt

½ cup / 120g mayonnaise

juice of 1 lemon

1 tsp black pepper

½ tsp salt

2 cloves of garlic, grated

TO SERVE

½ a head of lettuce, shredded

1 cucumber, chopped

1 large tomato, chopped

1 red onion, thinly sliced

a small handful of fresh parsley, roughly chopped

sriracha   ↔ your favorite hot sauce

Preheat the oven to 400°F / 200°C.

Cut the pitas into triangles and toss with 1 Tbsp oil and ½ tsp of the paprika.

On a baking sheet, combine the cauliflower, bell pepper, and chickpeas. Grate the garlic over the top, add the remaining 2 tsp paprika, the cumin, oregano, 1 tsp of salt, and the remaining 3 Tbsp of olive oil. Rub the spices into the cauliflower well and bake for 25 to 30 minutes until the cauliflower is cooked through.

Wash the rice and put it into a pan. Add water to the pan, filling to about 2 inches / 5cm above the rice, then add the turmeric and 1 tsp of salt, and bring to a boil. Once boiling, decrease the heat to low, put a lid on the pan, and set a timer for 10 minutes. Drain the rice and put it back into the pan with the lid off. Let steam until you're ready to eat.

Combine the ingredients for the sauce and add 3 to 4 Tbsp of water to thin it down if needed.

Serve the rice in bowls with the roasted veg, lettuce, cucumber, tomato, onion, parsley, and pita. Generously drizzle with the sauce and sriracha and serve.

> **COOKING RICE**
> When I cook rice I don't bother measuring the water. Just fill up the pot so it covers the rice by at least 2 inches / 5cm, cook for 10 minutes, and then drain all the water when it's done. Make sure to let the drained rice steam in the pot with the lid on to get it extra fluffy!

GREEN

ALL I WANT IS SOMETHING . . .

EGGPLANT & MUSHROOM ISKENDER

On all my many trips to Berlin my absolute favorite thing to eat was the iskender from Doyum, an incredible Turkish grillhouse (if you haven't tried this, please do!). Layers of crispy bread and spicy tomato, drizzled with lots of butter, usually topped with juicy lamb. I've got juicy mushrooms and eggplant in my recipe. All the veg and the croutons are roasted at the same time, so it comes together to make a very delicious weeknight meal. And if the length of the ingredients list is putting you off, I've used the same three spices several times, so it's not as many different ones as it seems!

1 large eggplant, cut into large chunks

8 oz / 225g white button or crimini mushrooms, halved

1 tsp garlic powder

½ tsp cumin seeds

1 tsp smoked paprika

1 tsp chili powder

1 tsp salt

1 Tbsp olive oil

2 vine-ripe tomatoes

FOR THE BREAD

10 oz / 280g crusty stale bread, torn into large chunks

1 Tbsp olive oil

1 tsp garlic powder

FOR THE TOMATO SAUCE

2 cloves of garlic, chopped

½ tsp cumin seeds

1 x 14-oz / 400g can of diced tomatoes

1 tsp chili powder

1 tsp smoked paprika

1 tsp za'atar   ↔ ½ tsp sumac and
                     ½ tsp sesame seeds

1 tsp salt

olive oil

FOR THE YOGURT

4 green onions, finely chopped

1 bunch of fresh parsley, finely chopped, plus more for serving

1¼ cups / 300g thick Greek yogurt

juice of 1 lemon

salt

TO ASSEMBLE

¼ cup / 55g unsalted butter

2 cloves of garlic

1 tsp smoked paprika

2 Tbsp sliced almonds

a squeeze of lemon juice

pickled chiles

GREEN

ALL I WANT IS SOMETHING . . .

Preheat the oven to 400°F / 200°C.

Put the eggplant and mushrooms into a bowl and add the dried spices, salt, and oil. Place them on a baking sheet along with the whole tomatoes and roast for 30 minutes, tossing halfway through, until crispy and charred.

Meanwhile, put the pieces of bread on another baking sheet. Drizzle with the oil and sprinkle with the garlic powder, then roast in the oven for 15 minutes, or until golden and crisp.

To make the tomato sauce, heat a glug of oil in a small pot and add the garlic and cumin seeds. Cook for 2 minutes, then add the canned tomatoes, chili powder, paprika, za'atar, and salt. Simmer for 15 minutes, then blend with an immersion blender.

Mix the green onions and parsley with the yogurt, lemon juice, and ½ tsp of salt. Add 2 to 3 Tbsp of water to loosen slightly.

To assemble, lay the croutons on your serving dish and top with the roasted eggplant and mushrooms. Layer the tomato sauce and yogurt mixture on top. Heat the butter in a small pan and grate in the garlic. Add the paprika and almonds, bring to a simmer, then when the almonds are slightly browned pour over the dish.

Sprinkle with more parsley and a squeeze of lemon juice, and serve with the roasted tomatoes and pickled chiles.

NOTE

→ *Sub in zucchini, or even lamb or chicken pieces roasted in the same spices.*

SUMAC & LIME OYSTER MUSHROOMS

This recipe is quite a special one. It's the last recipe I put in this book and it's only in here because I had a breakdown and wanted to reshoot the cover (days before the cover was due) and this recipe was the only one that would work for the vision I had, and so it was. I've had so many different versions of these mushrooms by now and they just keep getting better and better.

1 Tbsp garlic powder

1 Tbsp sumac

½ tsp sugar

1 cup / 140g all-purpose flour

3 eggs

3 cups / 180g panko breadcrumbs

8 oz / 225g oyster mushrooms

1 lime, for zesting

a small handful of parsley, finely chopped

peri peri sauce, for serving

vegetable oil, for frying

salt

Combine the garlic powder, sumac, 1 tsp of salt, and the sugar in a small bowl.

Heat a large pot of oil over medium-high heat for deep-frying.

Place the flour in a bowl, crack the eggs into another, lightly beat the eggs, and fill a third bowl with the panko. Season them all with salt.

Dunk the mushrooms in flour and then the eggs and finally press on the panko.

Deep-fry the mushrooms for 3 minutes until golden brown and crispy.

Toss them in the garlic-sumac salt, grate on lots of lime zest, and sprinkle with parsley.

Eat while still hot with a shake of peri peri sauce and enjoy the beautiful crunch.

NOTES

→   Use sumac from a Middle Eastern store; good-quality sumac makes a world of a difference. You can also switch up the seasoning to match whatever meal you're having.

→   Instead of the garlic and sumac mixture, try a mixture of Parmesan, garlic powder, and parsley, or even some of the secret spice mix from my recipe for Seema's Fried Chicken (page 165).

GREEN

ALL I WANT IS SOMETHING . . .

CABBAGE DUMPLINGS

Dumplings and cabbage rolls are a universal love language. Fillings wrapped in parcels can be found in cuisines all over the world – whether it's sarmale from Romania, kåldolmar from Sweden, or fagottini di verza from Italy, they are hard to resist. After eating numerous versions for my national dish series, here I've combined cabbage rolls with my love of dumplings. It's a simple yet deeply satisfying meal, brimming with hearty vegetables.

Feel free to make this dish completely vegetarian by swapping the chicken for crumbled tofu or using your favorite protein. You can also toss in any finely minced veggies, such as spinach, carrots, or celery. It's the perfect way to clean out your fridge.

GREEN

1 head of Napa cabbage ↔ Savoy cabbage or green cabbage

vegetable oil

FOR THE FILLING

8 oz / 225g white button mushrooms, finely chopped

4 green onions, finely chopped

12 oz / 340g ground chicken, ↔ any ground protein preferably dark meat

4 cloves of garlic, grated

3 Tbsp soy sauce

½ tsp red pepper flakes

1 Tbsp oyster sauce

1 Tbsp Shaoxing rice wine ↔ dry sherry, white wine, or mirin

1 Tbsp cornstarch

salt and black pepper

FOR THE DIPPING SAUCE

3 cloves of garlic, grated

1 green onion, finely chopped

1 Tbsp chili powder

1 Tbsp sesame seeds

½ cup / 120ml vegetable oil

2 Tbsp soy sauce

1 Tbsp Chinese black vinegar ↔ balsamic vinegar

Start by bringing a large pot of salted water to a boil. (This is the same pot you'll use for your steamer.) Peel the larger leaves off the cabbage, keeping the middle core with the small leaves for later. Boil the cabbage leaves for 1 minute, then rinse with cold water and set aside. Keep the hot water in the pan for later.

Finely chop the core of the cabbage and combine with the rest of the filling ingredients. Heat a little oil in a small skillet and cook 1 Tbsp of the filling. Taste and adjust the seasoning if needed.

Lay the cabbage leaves out on a work surface. Place 2 Tbsp of the filling on a leaf and roll it up like a burrito, folding in the sides. Continue with the rest of the cabbage leaves.

Put the cabbage rolls into a bamboo steamer lined with parchment paper and steam for about 15 minutes or until the filling is fully cooked.

To make the sauce, put the garlic and green onions into a bowl and add the chili powder and sesame seeds. In a small skillet heat the vegetable oil until it starts smoking. Add the garlic mixture and immediately turn off the heat. Stir well to ensure the garlic cooks evenly. Remove from the heat and add the soy sauce and vinegar.

Serve the cabbage rolls with the sauce poured on top and enjoy with steamed short-grain rice.

NOTES

→ *Don't have a bamboo steamer? Put a small bowl upside down in a large pot. Add just enough water to cover the bowl and place a plate that fits inside the pot on top. Line the plate with parchment paper and use this setup to steam your dumplings.*

→ *If you've got any oranges or similar fruits, zest some into the dipping sauce for a delightful zing.*

ALL I WANT IS SOMETHING . . .

JERK-SPICED BUTTER CAULIFLOWER & CRUNCHY MAPLE CHICKPEAS

I've always found cauliflower quite a tricky beast. I love the look of a whole roasted cauliflower, but the flavorless inside makes me a bit sad. So I've torn off large florets and rubbed every crevice with my spicy jerk butter. This packs a big punch, so don't miss out on the lemony yogurt underneath and the sweet maple chickpeas.

GREEN

FOR THE JERK BUTTER

3 green onions, roughly chopped

1 small onion, roughly chopped

6 cloves of garlic, chopped

2 inches / 5cm ginger, chopped

2 tsp dried thyme   ↔ rosemary
                             ∼ optional

1 Tbsp ground allspice

2 Tbsp white wine vinegar   ↔ apple cider vinegar

1 Tbsp maple syrup   ↔ honey

½ to 1 Scotch bonnet chile, stemmed

½ tsp ground cinnamon

¼ cup / 55g unsalted butter, softened

2 Tbsp soy sauce

1 tsp salt

1 head of cauliflower, cut into quarters, stem intact

1 x 14-oz / 400g can of chickpeas, drained

3 Tbsp unsweetened shredded coconut

3 Tbsp maple syrup   ↔ honey

½ tsp salt

1¼ cups / 300g unsweetened ↔ plain yogurt
coconut yogurt

juice of 1 lemon

Preheat the oven to 375°F / 190°C.

To make the jerk butter, blend all the ingredients in the food processor until smooth, using half the Scotch bonnet to start with. Give it a taste and add more Scotch bonnet a little at a time until you get the desired spiciness.

Put the cauliflower on a baking sheet and rub it liberally with the jerk butter, focusing on the florets. Roast for 30 minutes until cooked all the way through, basting every 10 minutes with the butter and making sure the cauliflower is well coated.

Combine the chickpeas with the shredded coconut, maple syrup, and salt. Spread on a second baking sheet and roast in the oven for 20 minutes until crispy, stirring halfway through.

Combine the yogurt and lemon juice.

Serve the buttery cauliflower on top of the yogurt with the crispy chickpeas alongside.

ALL I WANT IS SOMETHING …

NOTE
→   *Try serving this in a wrap or on thick flatbreads with a quick coleslaw.*

CARAMELIZED RED ONION & ZUCCHINI ORZO SALAD

There is a phrase, what grows together goes together, and that's very true for zucchini and corn. In this dish both are charred until blistered – times when I love my gas stove – and tossed with a really zesty sumac and caramelized onion dressing. The dressing is a nod to the flavors of glorious musakhan, the national dish of Palestine. There, chicken is bathed in a slowly cooked sea of onions, then generously dusted with more sumac than you'd think is appropriate. Yet it all comes together incredibly beautifully, just like this salad.

FOR THE DRESSING

2 red onions, thinly sliced   ↔ any onions

¼ cup / 60ml extra-virgin olive oil

4 cloves of garlic, finely chopped

½ tsp red pepper flakes

2 Tbsp sumac   ↔ 2 Tbsp za'atar and zest of 1 lime

juice of 2 lemons

1 tsp honey

⅛ tsp ground cumin

3 zucchini, halved lengthwise

2 ears of corn, husks removed

1¼ cups / 250g orzo

1½ cups / 200g frozen peas

a large handful of fresh mint, roughly chopped

2 oz / 55g feta

salt and black pepper

Put the onions into a heavy pan with the oil and a large pinch of salt and cook for 20 minutes over medium heat until jammy and caramelized. Set aside.

Meanwhile, crosshatch the cut sides of the zucchini halves and rub them with salt. Char the zucchini and corn on a grill pan until the zucchini have softened and the corn is charred, about 10 minutes. You can also use your gas burner, gently rotating them on the flame or under a very hot broiler.

Chop the zucchini into chunks and slice the corn kernels off the cobs.

Boil the orzo according to the package instructions, adding the peas for the last 2 minutes of cooking; drain.

Return the pan of onions to low heat and add the garlic, red pepper flakes, and sumac. Cook for 2 minutes, then remove from the heat and add the lemon juice, honey, cumin, and black pepper. Toss the dressing with the cooked veg, orzo, and mint, then crumble in the feta and adjust the seasoning.

STICKY UMAMI MUSHROOM RICE BOWL

Does a mushroom count as a vegetable? Anyway, one of my ultimate comfort foods is buttery soy sauce rice. Trust me, hot rice with a salted butter and soy sauce is insanely delicious. I've kept the umaminess of butter and soy and topped it with some crispy charred mushrooms for an incredibly satisfying bowl of rice. Then it's all fused together with a creamy egg yolk for some extra richness.

GREEN

FOR THE STICKY MUSHROOMS

¼ cup / 55g salted butter

1 Tbsp oyster sauce ↔ veggie oyster sauce

¼ cup / 60ml soy sauce

1 lb / 450g oyster mushrooms

8 oz / 225g firm tofu, cut into small cubes

1 tsp cornstarch

2 tsp toasted sesame oil

4 egg yolks

FOR THE RICE

3 green onions, roughly chopped

2 shallots, finely chopped

6 cloves of garlic, roughly chopped

1½ inches / 4cm ginger, grated

2 cups / 400g sushi rice ↔ any short-grain rice

2¼ cups / 500ml vegetable stock

2 Tbsp Shaoxing rice wine ↔ dry sherry, mirin, or sake

1 tsp salt

vegetable oil

Preheat the broiler to its hottest setting.

Melt the butter in the microwave and combine in a large bowl with the oyster sauce, soy sauce, and 6 Tbsp / 90ml of water.

Add the mushrooms and tofu to the bowl and massage them well so they absorb some of the liquid.

Reserve some of the green onions for garnish and put the rest into a heavy pan with the shallots, garlic, ginger, and a large glug of oil. Fry for 5 minutes until softened.

Wash your rice until the water runs clear. Add the rice to the pan with the shallot mixture along with the stock, Shaoxing wine, and salt. Bring to a simmer, then decrease the heat to low and put a lid on. Cook for 15 minutes, then turn off the heat and let the rice steam for 10 minutes.

Meanwhile, place the mushrooms and tofu on a baking sheet, reserving the liquid, and broil for 25 to 30 minutes or until charred. Set aside.

Put the reserved mushroom liquid into a medium pan and bring to a boil. Make a slurry with the cornstarch and 2 Tbsp of water, then add to the mushroom liquid to thicken. Toss the mushrooms and tofu in the liquid and remove the pan from the heat.

Divide the sticky mushrooms and tofu among four serving bowls and fill the rest of the bowls with rice.

Turn each bowl upside down onto a plate to unveil the mushroom domes. Brush with the sesame oil and top each with an egg yolk and the chopped reserved green onions and enjoy.

NOTE
→ Use whatever mushrooms you have. If they are chestnut or button mushrooms, tear them up with your hands so they get more crispy. But as a treat, oyster mushrooms have a meatiness that works fantastically here!

CRUNCHY COCONUT & SESAME BROCCOLINI

Any time I need a quick green side for a meal, this is my go-to. It goes with everything, looks quite special, and tastes fantastic. The simple sesame sauce is based on a traditional Japanese goma sauce, using tahini as a quick hack. And the crunchy coconut topping is inspired by the many coconut chutneys I had in Kerala. You can even cheat and just mix toasted coconut into your favorite chili crisp – I promise not to tell anyone!

This is great as a quick lunch over rice.

1 lb / 450g broccolini, thick stems sliced in half lengthwise

salt

FOR THE SESAME SAUCE

¼ cup / 70g tahini	↔ 2 Tbsp of any nut butter
¼ cup / 60ml unseasoned rice vinegar	↔ white wine vinegar

1 tsp soy sauce

2 tsp brown sugar

1 tsp toasted sesame oil

5 Tbsp / 75ml hot water

¼ tsp salt

FOR THE CRUNCHY COCONUT TOPPING

2 Tbsp peanuts

2 Tbsp unsweetened shredded coconut

¼ cup / 60ml vegetable oil

1 Tbsp red pepper flakes

2 Tbsp crispy shallots	↔ onions (see note)

salt

Cook the broccolini in heavily salted boiling water for 4 to 5 minutes until tender.

Meanwhile, combine all the ingredients for the sesame sauce. When you add the water it will start to clump up, but continue whisking in more water until it's a smooth sauce. Season with salt.

Roughly chop the peanuts and toast in a pan with the coconut until golden. Add the oil and red pepper flakes. Once the pepper flakes start to fizz, cook for another 30 seconds and then turn off the heat. Transfer the peanuts, coconut, and shallots to a bowl and add ½ tsp of salt.

Lay the broccolini on a plate and drizzle with the sesame sauce. Sprinkle with the crunchy coconut mixture and serve.

NOTES

→   Cook your broccolini any way you want – keep it simple by just boiling or steaming, roast it in a fiery hot oven, or blanch it quickly in water and char it in a hot pan.

→   I'm using store-bought fried shallots/onions, which I always keep in my pantry, but if you want to make your own, you can thinly slice them, lightly toss them in flour, and fry them in a few tablespoons of oil until golden and crispy.

→   This works great for any green veg! Try it with some bok choy or just lots of wilted spinach.

THAI BASIL EGGPLANT

Herbs are far more than just a garnish, and recipes like this really showcase them. This recipe is all about celebrating the herbal glory of basil. You'll want to use enough basil so that it takes center stage in your dish, much like you would with spinach.

This creation draws inspiration from fiery Thai basil chicken, a super-spicy and fragrant dish, but I've used caramelized onions to mellow out the heat from those fiery peppers.

4 Tbsp olive oil

2 large eggplants, cut into thick wedges

3 small onions, sliced

5 cloves of garlic, finely chopped

3 Thai red chiles (small ones), stemmed and finely minced   ↔ 4 long red chiles or 1 tsp red pepper flakes

3 Tbsp soy sauce

1 Tbsp oyster sauce   ↔ veggie oyster sauce

1¼ cups / 200g cherry tomatoes, halved

2 large handfuls of Thai basil (about 3½ oz / 100g), leaves picked   ↔ regular basil

salt

Heat 2 Tbsp of the oil in a wok over medium heat and fry the eggplant pieces on all sides until they turn a glorious golden color. Once done, remove from the wok and set aside.

Add the remaining 2 Tbsp of oil to the wok. Toss in the onions and let them cook slowly for 20 minutes until they become soft and wonderfully caramelized.

Stir in the garlic and chiles, letting them sizzle for another 2 minutes.

Return the eggplant to the wok and add the soy sauce, oyster sauce, tomatoes, and ½ cup / 120ml of water. Let it all simmer together for 15 minutes, allowing the sauce to thicken and the eggplant to become tender. If things look a bit dry, add a splash of water.

Finally, add the basil leaves and toss until they wilt. Season with a pinch of salt and serve on a bed of fluffy rice.

GREEN

ALL I WANT IS SOMETHING …

NOTE

→   When working with hot chiles, it's best to blend them or use a mortar and pestle to avoid any unexpected bursts of spicy heat in your mouth. If you prefer a milder kick, go for just two long red chiles.

122

SOMETHING COMFORTING

CITRUSY MISO ROAST CHICKEN WITH PICKLED CHILE & CHIVE DRESSING

Roast chicken has always been one of my favorite things on the planet, and in this recipe, which takes inspiration from Ottolenghi's miso butter onions, the miso gives it a buttery, savory boost and the citrus cuts through the richness. When topped with the vinegary dressing my brother said it was the nicest roast chicken he'd ever had.

1 (2 lb / 900g) whole chicken

14 oz / 400g shallots,   ↔ white onions, halved
peeled and left whole

1.3 lb / 600g baby potatoes

¼ cup / 55g unsalted butter

1 orange, cut into wedges, for serving

1 lime, cut into wedges, for serving

FOR THE MARINADE

juice of 1 orange

juice of 2 lemons

juice of 1 lime   ⁓ optional

6 cloves of garlic, crushed

2 Tbsp brown sugar

2 Tbsp miso paste

1 Tbsp dried tarragon   ↔ sage or oregano

1 Tbsp coriander seeds, crushed

FOR THE PICKLED GREEN CHILE & CHIVE DRESSING

1 bunch of fresh chives,   ↔ green onions
finely chopped

3 green chiles, stemmed and roughly chopped

½ tsp salt

3 cloves of garlic, chopped

2 Tbsp sesame seeds

scant ½ cup / 100ml vegetable oil

2 Tbsp unseasoned rice   ↔ apple cider vinegar
vinegar

Preheat the oven to 395°F / 200°C (this may seem high, but spatchcocked chicken cooks much faster).

Using a pair of kitchen shears, cut the backbone out of the chicken. Flip it over and press firmly on the breast to flatten the chicken, then turn out the legs so they are facing outwards.

For the marinade, put the citrus juices into a large bowl. Add the garlic, brown sugar, miso, tarragon, and coriander seeds.

Place the chicken in the marinade, skin-side down, and marinate for 30 minutes to 1 hour (but no longer, as the citrus can start to cure the chicken).

Place the shallots and potatoes on a large baking sheet and dot with knobs of the butter. Put the chicken on top of the potatoes skin-side up and pour the marinade over the top.

Roast in the oven for 45 minutes, basting with the marinade every 15 minutes.

Once the chicken is cooked and the juices run clear, remove from the oven and place on a carving board. Let rest for 15 minutes. Meanwhile, return the potatoes and shallots to the oven for another 15 minutes to crisp up.

To make the dressing, place the chives in a heatproof bowl and set aside.

Pound the chiles, salt, and garlic in a mortar and pestle.

Toast the sesame seeds in a small pan until golden, then add the oil and the pounded garlic mixture. Let sizzle for 2 minutes, then pour it over the chives in the bowl and stir in the vinegar.

Once the chicken has rested, slice it into thighs, legs, wings, and breasts. Serve on top of the potatoes and shallots with the tangy chive dressing spooned on top and orange and lime wedges alongside for squeezing.

COMFORTING

ALL I WANT IS SOMETHING ...

FRENCH ONION GNOCCHI

When it comes to winter soups, French onion reigns as the undisputed king. The slow caramelization of the onions is a labor of love in itself, resulting in a deep, rich flavor that's worth every minute. In this recipe, those beautifully caramelized onions are paired with tender gnocchi, all swimming in a hearty stock infused with the umami goodness of miso and earthy mushrooms. It's the kind of comforting meal that warms you from the inside out.

Make this completely veggie by leaving out the Worcestershire sauce.

8 oz / 225g chestnut or crimini mushrooms, sliced	
1 lb / 450g onions, thinly sliced	
1 vegetable stock cube	
1 Tbsp miso paste	⌁ optional
1 Tbsp Worcestershire sauce	↔ use 1 anchovy, or omit
1 Tbsp balsamic vinegar	↔ white wine vinegar or red wine vinegar
6 cloves of garlic, finely chopped	
¼ cup / 55g unsalted butter	
½ tsp dried thyme	↔ dried rosemary
⅔ cup / 160ml dry white wine	↔ chicken or vegetable stock, plus 2 Tbsp white wine vinegar
1 lb / 450g potato gnocchi	
4 oz / 115g Gruyère cheese	↔ any melty cheese
¾ cup / 45g panko breadcrumbs	
2 oz / 55g Parmesan, grated (about 1 cup)	↔ veggie Parmesan or other hard cheese
olive oil	
salt	

In a dry pan over medium heat cook the mushrooms with a pinch of salt for about 10 minutes. The water in the mushrooms will evaporate first, and once they're dry and start sticking to the pan add 1 Tbsp of oil and cook for another 3 minutes over high heat until crispy. Transfer them to a bowl.

Using the same pan (no need to clean it), cook the onions with a generous amount of oil over medium heat for 25 minutes until they are very caramelized. Add 1 Tbsp of water if the pan looks dry and continue cooking.

Preheat the oven to 375°F / 190°C.

Crumble the vegetable stock cube into a bowl and add the miso, if using, Worcestershire sauce, and vinegar. Stir in 2 cups / 475ml of boiling water to dissolve the stock cube.

Add the garlic, butter, and thyme to the onions and cook for 2 minutes, then deglaze with the wine. Bring to a simmer, then add the vegetable stock mixture, cooked mushrooms, and gnocchi. Stir and cook for 10 minutes until the sauce thickens.

Grate half the Gruyère and roughly chop the rest. Mix the roughly chopped cheese into the gnocchi.

Transfer the gnocchi mixture to a 10-inch / 25cm baking dish and top it with the panko, grated Gruyère, and Parmesan. Bake for about 15 minutes or until it turns golden and crispy.

ALL I WANT IS SOMETHING …

CHEAT'S CURRIED OMURICE

If you've fallen down the rabbit hole of TikTok and witnessed the glorious cascading scrambled egg pocket, chances are you've encountered the legend himself, Chef Motokichi Yukimura, the Omurice maestro from Kichi Kichi Omurice. It fueled my obsession, but despite how easy he makes it look, it's not. And so that you don't need to feel my disappointment, I've developed a cheat's version that gets you 85 percent there with 10 percent of the fuss. Then it's smothered in a quick curry sauce that hits all the spots without the heartache.

FOR THE CILANTRO–GREEN ONION RICE

1½ cups / 300g sushi rice

1 vegetable stock cube ↔ chicken stock cube

2 green onions, finely chopped

1 tsp dark soy sauce

a small handful of fresh cilantro, finely chopped

FOR THE CURRY SAUCE

1 carrot, grated

1 onion, grated

1 tsp grated fresh ginger

2 cloves of garlic, grated

1 tsp curry powder

½ tsp garam masala ⸺ optional

½ tsp chili powder

1 Tbsp all-purpose flour

2 Tbsp soy sauce

1 Tbsp honey

vegetable oil

salt

FOR THE EGGS

4 eggs

2 Tbsp unsalted butter

Wash the rice three times until the water runs almost clear, then drain.

Dissolve the vegetable stock cube in 1⅔ cups / 400ml of water.

Put the rice into a pan with the green onions, vegetable stock, and dark soy. Bring to a simmer, then decrease the heat to low, put a lid on, and cook for 10 minutes. Once cooked, let rest for 5 minutes then mix in the chopped cilantro.

To make the curry sauce, heat a glug of oil in a pan and add the carrot, onion, ginger, and garlic. Sauté for 5 minutes until softened.

Add the curry powder, garam masala, if using, and chili powder and cook for 2 minutes. Stir in the flour and cook for 2 minutes, then slowly pour in 1⅔ cups / 395ml of water, mixing well.

Add the soy sauce and honey and bring to a simmer. Season with salt.

To cook the eggs, place the smallest nonstick skillet you have on the lowest heat setting. Crack in 2 eggs (you must do this one serving at a time) and add half the butter. Very gently scramble together over low heat, using a spatula to make soft-set eggs. Fold the eggs over each other, making small curds. Once the eggs are three-quarters cooked, turn off the heat and allow the bottom to set slightly; repeat with the remaining eggs and butter.

To serve, fill a bowl with the rice and tip it upside down onto a plate to make a dome. Place the egg on top of the dome and spoon on the curry sauce.

NOTES

→ *If you can find those Japanese curry blocks you can use 2 cubes instead of the spices, flour, and honey for a rapid curry sauce.*

→ *This is great for using up leftover rice – you can stir-fry it with garlic and green onion, or double up on the egg for an egg-fried rice!*

FEEL BETTER GINGER & LIME CHICKEN SOUP

My ultimate comfort food is always soup. It's warming, comforting, and has this undeniable power to wrap you up in a blanket. For when you're not feeling too well, I've developed this simple soup that will get you back in action in no time. It also freezes well without the pasta so you can have it ready for some really sniffly emergencies.

1 onion, finely chopped

1 carrot, finely chopped

5 cloves of garlic, thinly sliced

2 inches / 5cm ginger, half grated, half finely chopped

½ tsp ground turmeric

1 tsp black peppercorns

1 tsp coriander seeds	↔ try cumin seeds instead!
1 whole chicken	↔ 4 bone-in chicken thighs

½ head of cabbage

8 oz / 225g small pasta (I keep alphabet pasta for emergencies)	↔ egg noodles

2 green chiles, stemmed and chopped

1 bunch of green onions, chopped

a small handful of fresh cilantro, chopped

juice of 2 limes

¼ cup / 60g full-fat yogurt, for serving

vegetable oil

salt

Heat a big glug of oil in a large stockpot. Add the onion, carrot, garlic, and grated ginger. Sauté for 3 minutes, then add the turmeric, peppercorns, coriander seeds, and chicken. Pour in cold water so that the chicken is covered. Bring to a simmer and cook over low heat for 45 minutes.

Remove the chicken from the pot and shred the cooked meat, discarding the skin and bones (or for an extra chickeny broth, see notes).

Roughly chop the cabbage and add it to the soup. Cook for 10 minutes. In a separate pot, cook the pasta according to package instructions.

Meanwhile, combine the chopped ginger, chiles, and most of the green onions and cilantro in a heatproof bowl. Heat up ¼ cup / 60ml of oil and pour this over the green onion–ginger mixture. Squeeze in the lime juice, then taste and season generously with 1 tsp of salt.

Plate up your soup with pieces of chicken and cooked pasta, then sprinkle with the reserved cilantro and green onions, dollop on the yogurt, and drizzle with the green onion oil.

NOTES

→   For an extra intense chickeny flavor roast the bones with a bit of oil at 400°F / 200°C until dark golden, then put them back in the soup to simmer for another hour.

→   I love how the yogurt adds some freshness to the soup, but you can also use a drizzle of cream if yogurt's not your thing.

COMFORTING

ALL I WANT IS SOMETHING ...

CREAMY PAPRIKASH BEANS

I'm always intrigued by the simplicity of staple home dishes around the world. Hungarian paprikash is no exception, the star of the show being their beloved paprika flavoring a thick chicken stew. Hungarian paprika is far superior to our supermarket version, but I've used the essence of the dish to make these delightfully creamy beans, perfect for scooping with crusty bread.

This would be great paired with crunchy roasted potatoes (try my garlicky anchovy butter smashed potatoes on page 56).

1 onion, finely chopped

1 red bell pepper, stemmed, seeded, and finely chopped

5 cloves of garlic, finely chopped

1 tsp red pepper flakes

2 Tbsp tomato paste

2 Tbsp smoked paprika

1 Tbsp apple cider vinegar

6 Tbsp / 90ml heavy cream

1 x 14-oz / 400g can of butter beans or cannellini beans

olive oil

salt and black pepper

TO SERVE

2 oz / 55g feta, crumbled (about ½ cup)

a small handful of fresh basil

½ tsp red pepper flakes

4 slices of crusty bread

Sauté the onion, bell pepper, garlic, and red pepper flakes with a glug of oil in a pan for 10 minutes until soft.

Add the tomato paste and cook for another 5 minutes until darkened. Add the paprika, vinegar, cream, and beans, including the liquid from the can.

Mix well and bring to a simmer, then cook for 5 minutes until warmed through and thick. Season generously with salt and pepper.

To serve, sprinkle with the feta, basil leaves, and red pepper flakes. Drizzle with olive oil and enjoy with slices of crusty bread.

COMFORTING

ALL I WANT IS SOMETHING ...

SEB'S TARRAGON CHICKEN

One of the most comforting foods for me is chicken, and this chicken is one of the best I've had. Seb, my partner, made it for me when I first visited his family home in Sweden – he picked all the herbs from his mum's garden, grilled the chicken on their woodfired grill, and packed it with garlic just the way I like. The way to my heart is chicken, and I hope this chicken makes its way into yours.

COMFORTING

a large handful of fresh tarragon, finely chopped

3 cloves of garlic, finely chopped

a small handful of fresh oregano, finely chopped ←→ parsley, chives, or thyme

1 lemon, halved

¼ cup / 60ml extra-virgin olive oil

½ tsp salt

1 tsp coarsely ground black pepper

4 bone-in, skin-on chicken thighs

TO FINISH

2 cloves of garlic, thinly sliced

2 Tbsp unsalted butter

flaky salt

Put 2 Tbsp of the tarragon into a large bowl along with the chopped garlic, oregano, juice of ½ the lemon, the oil, salt, pepper, and chicken thighs.

Marinate for 20 minutes (optional, or while you heat the grill, if using).

Heat a cast-iron skillet over medium heat. Brush most of the marinade off the chicken, reserving it for later, and cook skin-side down for 7 minutes until golden and crisp.

Turn the chicken over and continue cooking for 4 to 5 minutes. Remove and let rest on your serving plate.

Add the reserved marinade, sliced garlic, butter, and 2 Tbsp water to the pan and boil for 2 to 3 minutes until fragrant. Turn off the heat and stir in the remaining tarragon.

Pour the buttery tarragon mixture over the chicken. Squeeze on the juice of the remaining ½ lemon, sprinkle with flaky sea salt, and serve.

NOTES

→   *This is a perfect summer grilling recipe: grill the chicken on the grate and cook the marinade with the butter in a pan. Serve with some grilled potatoes to soak up the butter.*

→   *If you want to get fancy and make for easier eating, bone the chicken – make sure to reduce the cooking time by half if you do so.*

MISO MUSHROOM CARBONARA-ESQUE SPAGHETTI

Creamy mushroom pasta has always been my favorite, but there are just never enough mushrooms for me, and the addition of cream can make the pasta feel too heavy. I've loaded this recipe with mushrooms so you really get a mouthful per bite. The meatiness of the mushrooms plus a dash of miso paste makes this veggie "carbonara-style" pasta, where I use the egg yolks and Pecorino to make a lusciously creamy sauce.

12 oz / 340g mixed mushrooms

½ tsp red pepper flakes

1½ tsp coarsely ground black pepper, plus more for serving

8 oz / 225g spaghetti

2½ oz / 75g Pecorino, plus more for serving   ← veggie Pecorino or other hard cheese

3 egg yolks

1 Tbsp white miso paste

6 cloves of garlic, thinly sliced

extra-virgin olive oil

salt

Tear the mushrooms, add to a large, dry pan with ½ tsp of salt, and cook for 10 minutes over medium-high heat until all the water has evaporated and the mushrooms start to brown. Add a large glug of oil, the red pepper flakes, and black pepper and brown the mushrooms for 5 minutes.

Cook your spaghetti in a large pot of lightly salted boiling water according to the package instructions. Remove the pasta with tongs to a separate bowl, keeping the pasta water in the pot to boil.

Grate the Pecorino using the star side of the box grater – or blitz to dust in a food processor. This makes it easier to melt it into the sauce. In a heatproof bowl whisk the Pecorino, egg yolks, and miso with ½ cup / 120ml of pasta cooking water.

Add another glug of oil to the mushroom pan. Add the garlic and cook for 5 minutes, then add a splash of pasta water to stop the cooking.

Turn off the heat and add the cooked spaghetti and the egg yolk mixture. Place the bowl over the boiling pasta water and mix vigorously until it's all emulsified, adding more pasta water as needed to make a thick, glossy sauce.

Serve with more grated Pecorino and black pepper.

CRISPY CHILI-GARLIC ROAST POTATOES

I'm not the biggest fan of potatoes – they need to be perfectly crispy and saucy so that I don't get that stodgy feeling in my throat. These potatoes are wonderfully crisp and tossed in an Indo-Chinese-style sticky sauce. Indo-Chinese is the melding of Indian and Chinese food, using the savoriness of soy sauce with the rich Indian spices. They would go great with any spicy main, or just as is, dunked in some yogurt.

2 lb / 900g potatoes, peeled and cut into large chunks

6 Tbsp / 90ml ghee   ↔ vegetable oil

1 Tbsp all-purpose flour

1 large onion, finely chopped

8 cloves of garlic, finely chopped

2 tsp chili powder

1 tsp ground coriander

1 tsp ground cumin

6 Tbsp / 100g ketchup

6 Tbsp / 90ml soy sauce

1 Tbsp chopped fresh cilantro

¾ cup / 180g thick Greek yogurt

salt

Preheat the oven to 400°F / 200°C.

Pop your potatoes into a pan of salted cold water, bring to a boil, and cook for 15 minutes or until just fork-tender.

Meanwhile, pour ¼ cup / 60ml of the oil onto a large baking sheet and place it in the oven to heat for 10 minutes.

Drain the potatoes and put them back into the pan. Add the flour, then put the lid on the pan and shake to fluff them up.

Take the hot baking sheet out of the oven and immediately pour the potatoes onto it so they sizzle. Toss the potatoes in the oil and roast in the oven for 45 minutes, turning halfway, until they are very crispy.

For the sauce, put the onion and garlic into a pan with the remaining 2 Tbsp of oil and fry for 5 minutes until soft and translucent. Add the chili powder, coriander, and cumin and cook for 1 minute. Stir in the ketchup and soy sauce and turn off the heat.

Once the potatoes are crispy toss them with the sauce, sprinkle with the cilantro, and serve with the yogurt.

COMFORTING

ALL I WANT IS SOMETHING ...

ZA'ATAR RICOTTA DUMPLINGS

Ricotta gnudi are a beloved Italian comfort food, and my twist on these soft, pillowy dumplings takes them to another level. They're coated in a garlicky Parmesan sauce and drizzled with a fresh, zesty, zhoug-like dressing. (Zhoug is a spicy cardamom and cilantro dressing from Yemen!) You can whip up this delightful dish in less than 30 minutes, making it perfect for any busy weeknight.

FOR THE RICOTTA GNUDI

1¼ cups / 300g ricotta

1 egg

1 cup / 140g all-purpose flour, plus more for rolling

2 oz / 55g Parmesan, grated (about 1 cup) ↔ veggie Parmesan or other hard cheese

2 Tbsp za'atar

1 tsp salt, plus more for salting the water

½ tsp freshly ground black pepper

FOR THE ZHOUG-LIKE DRESSING

a large handful of fresh parsley

2 green chiles, stemmed

1 Tbsp za'atar

juice of ½ a lemon

¼ cup / 60ml extra-virgin olive oil, plus more for drizzling

FOR THE PARMESAN SAUCE

1 shallot, finely chopped

2 Tbsp unsalted butter

6 cloves of garlic, thinly sliced

⅔ cup / 160ml dry white wine ↔ low-sodium chicken or vegetable stock

6 Tbsp / 90ml heavy cream

2 oz / 55g Parmesan, grated (about 1 cup) ↔ veggie Parmesan or other hard cheese

Strain the ricotta by pressing it in a sieve over a bowl to remove the excess water.

In a mixing bowl whisk the ricotta and egg until smooth, then add the flour, Parmesan, za'atar, salt, and pepper and stir to form a slightly sticky dough.

Place a few Tbsp of flour in a bowl. Roll small balls of dough in your hand, coat them in the flour, and make an indentation with your thumb in the middle. Use more flour if needed. Repeat with the rest of the dough and arrange the gnudi on a floured baking sheet.

Bring a large pot of lightly salted water to a boil.

For the zhoug-like dressing, blend the parsley, chiles, za'atar, and lemon juice in a mini food processor or with a mortar and pestle then slowly drizzle in the oil while blending until you have a smooth dressing. Set aside.

In a saucepan over medium heat, cook the shallot with the butter for 3 to 5 minutes until softened. Add the garlic and cook for 1 to 2 more minutes. Deglaze with the wine and bring to a boil. Stir in the cream and Parmesan, then decrease the heat.

Drop the gnudi into the boiling water and cook until they float to the surface, 1 to 3 minutes, depending on size. Transfer them to the Parmesan sauce and gently toss to combine, adding some cooking water if the sauce is too thick.

Serve the gnudi with the spicy zhoug-like dressing and a drizzle of olive oil.

NOTES

→   Try out other spice mixes, such as ras el hanout or even Old Bay seasoning, if you don't have any za'atar.

→   Raid your fridge for any extra herbs such as basil or cilantro to toss into the dressing. If you happen to have some olives on hand they'd also make a fantastic addition.

COMFORTING

ALL I WANT IS SOMETHING . . .

PICKLED JALAPEÑO MAC & CHEESE

Mac and cheese is universally known as comfort food. I've combined it with one of my other comforts, cheesy jalapeño nachos from the movie theater, making this one of the greatest things you can eat while watching a movie in bed. The secret is the one and only plastic cheese, which gives it that signature flavor. Generously topped with crispy onions, because you deserve it.

1 lb / 450g macaroni — any short pasta shape

¼ cup / 55g unsalted butter — vegetable oil

⅓ cup / 45g all-purpose flour

3 cups / 720ml milk — oat milk

7 oz / 200g aged Cheddar, grated (a scant 2 cups) — any cheeses you have

3½ oz / 100g red Leicester, grated (a scant 1 cup)

5 slices American cheese (the more processed, the better)

¾ cup / 90g pickled jalapeños, finely chopped — any pickles from the fridge

6 Tbsp / 90ml pickling liquid from the jalapeño jar

salt and black pepper

FOR THE TOPPING

1½ cups / 45g tortilla chips, crushed — breadcrumbs

¾ cup / 40g crispy shallots or onions

2 oz / 55g Parmesan cheese, grated (about 1 cup) — veggie Parmesan or other hard cheese

Preheat the oven to 350°F / 175°C.

Cook the macaroni in lightly salted boiling water for about 10 minutes, or a few minutes less than the recommended cooking time on the package. It will finish cooking in the sauce in the oven.

Melt the butter in a large saucepan and stir in the flour. Cook this mixture over medium-high heat for about 2 minutes. Then slowly drizzle in the milk in three additions, making sure to whisk well after each addition.

Add the Cheddar, red Leicester, and American cheeses, and mix until all the cheese has melted. Add the cooked pasta, jalapeños, and pickling liquid. Stir everything together and season with salt and pepper.

Pour the cheesy pasta mixture into a large baking dish and top with the crushed tortilla chips, crispy shallots, and Parmesan.

Bake for 20 minutes or until golden and bubbling. Allow to rest for 5 minutes and enjoy.

NOTES

→ Be sure to check the net weight of the jar of jalapeños to ensure you have enough for the recipe!

→ When it comes to cheese, let your creativity run wild. This recipe is fantastic for using up those little remnants hiding at the back of your fridge. Start with aged Cheddar as your base and throw in whatever other cheeses you have on hand. It's all about making it your own!

ALL I WANT IS SOMETHING …

TIME
2 HOURS

MAKES
ABOUT 15 ROTLI
(TO SERVE ABOUT 3 TO 4 PEOPLE)

VEGGIE

ROTLI

Rotli is something I am very fussy about. They need to be hot, soft, and very thin. Try one freshly cooked with lots of butter and you will understand my fussiness. My mum's recipe means they stay soft for days – her secret is to use hot water. Chapati flour also helps the rotlis puff up in that iconic ball, but if you don't have any, use whole-wheat or even all-purpose flour.

2¼ cups / 315g chapati flour, or 1¼ cups / 175g all-purpose flour plus 1 cup / 140g whole-wheat flour, plus more for dusting

½ tsp of salt

2 Tbsp vegetable oil

¾ cup plus 2 Tbsp / 205ml boiling water

In a bowl combine the flour, salt, 1 Tbsp of the oil, and the boiling water. Mix it with a spoon until it's cool enough to handle, then knead for 5 minutes to form a sticky dough. Pour the remaining 1 Tbsp of oil over the dough and continue to knead so that the dough is less sticky and very soft.

Cover the dough and allow it to rest for 15 to 20 minutes.

Place a skillet over high heat and allow it to warm up for 2 minutes.

Pinch off a golf ball–size piece of dough and liberally dust your work surface with flour. Roll the dough gently into a small circle and coat it again with flour. Continue rolling until you form a thin circle about 6 inches / 15cm in diameter.

Pick up the rotli and flip it over so the side you were just rolling is face down in the skillet. Cook for 30 seconds, until small bubbles appear, and then flip it. Cook for another 30 seconds and flip again. Then, using a clean kitchen towel, press down on the rotli. This will help it to puff up – press down on the parts that are puffing up to push the air to the sides of the rotli.

While one rotli is cooking, roll out the next one – bring in a friend to help you. Transfer the cooked rotli to a towel-lined dish to keep them warm. Continue rolling and cooking the rotli until you have run out of dough.

Enjoy with a curry, or even spread with butter and sprinkled with sugar as a snack.

ALL I WANT IS SOMETHING …

PEA & POTATO CURRY

A home-cooked classic for me is potato and pea curry. It's a dish you wouldn't normally see being served in Indian restaurants, but that's how you know it's one of the good ones. For me there are always peas in the freezer and potatoes somewhere in the pantry. The curry takes less than 30 minutes to make and is one of the most comforting meals on a cold day. Have this with rice or rotli.

3 inches / 7.5cm ginger, roughly chopped

7 cloves of garlic, roughly chopped

1 cup / 240g canned tomatoes (whole or chopped)

½ tsp cumin seeds

2 tsp chili powder

1 tsp ground cumin

1 tsp ground coriander

¼ tsp ground turmeric

1 lb / 450g potatoes, peeled and cut into large chunks

1½ cups / 200g frozen peas

a small handful of fresh cilantro, chopped, for serving

1 tsp salt

vegetable oil

Blitz together the ginger, garlic, and tomatoes in the food processor.

Heat a large glug of oil in a large pan and add the cumin seeds. Once they start to sizzle, pour in the blended tomato sauce.

Add the chili powder, ground cumin, coriander, turmeric, and salt and mix well.

Add the potatoes, then pour in 1 cup / 240ml of water and let this simmer for 15 to 20 minutes until the sauce is thick and the potatoes are cooked through.

Add the peas, then squish some of the potatoes against the side of the pan to thicken the curry. Cook for another 5 minutes.

Finish with the chopped cilantro and serve.

COMFORTING

CHAAS (SALTY LASSI)
A meal at my mum's was not complete without chaas (salty lassi). It's salty, savory, and perfect with any curry. Simply whisk together ⅔ cup / 160g yogurt, ¾ cup / 175ml cold water, ¼ tsp toasted and crushed cumin seeds, and ¼ tsp of salt.

LEFTOVERS
→   *If you have leftovers, this makes the best grilled cheese filling ever! Pile it up on bread with some cheese and cilantro chutney for a fantastic lunch!*

ALL I WANT IS SOMETHING . . .

CACIO E PEPE SCISSOR-CUT PASTA

This is a fantastic hack for creating a dish with the feeling of homemade pasta when in fact it takes about 30 minutes. I had the idea when I was seeing Chinese scissor-cut noodles along with a German technique for making spätzle. You use this with an Italian pasta dough and then combined with an Italian sauce it will feel like fresh homemade pasta with no fuss. It's one of my proudest creations and now you can see it all over the internet!

¾ cup / 105g all-purpose flour	↔ 00 flour
1 egg	
coarsely ground black pepper	
2 oz / 55g Pecorino, grated (about 1 cup), plus more for serving	↔ veggie Pecorino or other hard cheese
salt	

Combine the flour with the egg and a pinch of salt and knead for 5 to 8 minutes to form a soft dough. Cover with plastic wrap and rest for 15 (and up to 30) minutes.

Bring a pot of salted water to a boil.

Using a pair of clean kitchen shears, snip very small, thin pieces of the dough ball directly into the water. Cook for 2 to 3 minutes, until floating, then drain, reserving some of the pasta water.

Warm a pan over low heat and grind in 1 tsp of pepper. Toast for 1 minute, then ladle in ⅔ cup / 160ml of the reserved pasta water. Add the cooked pasta and then sprinkle with the Pecorino. Let sit for 30 seconds without stirring until the cheese melts, then toss the sauce and pasta together so the sauce coats the pasta.

Plate up with extra black pepper and Pecorino and enjoy.

NOTE
→   Use this technique to make fresh pasta for any pasta dish! I love it with a simple tomato sauce, too.

COMFORTING

ALL I WANT IS SOMETHING …

154

ALL I WANT IS ...

SOMETHING SPECIAL

THE BUTTER CHICKEN

Of all the recipes I've ever cooked, this one holds a special place in my heart, and for good reason. This isn't your run-of-the-mill creamy, mildly sweet butter chicken. The sauce is rich, and it's got a kick that will wake you up a bit. It doesn't really fit the traditional butter chicken mold, and there isn't a cashew in sight, but that's what makes it so special. This recipe has left an indelible mark on my life and culinary journey, and it's easily what I've become best known for, so naturally it was a must-have in this book.

FOR THE GARLIC, GINGER & CHILE PASTE

10 cloves of garlic

4 inches / 10cm ginger

6 to 10 green chiles

FOR THE CHICKEN MARINADE

⅔ cup / 160g plain full-fat yogurt (must be full-fat!)

juice of ½ a lemon

1 tsp chili powder

½ tsp ground turmeric

1 tsp ground cumin

1 tsp ground coriander

½ tsp garam masala

1¾ lb / 800g boneless, skinless chicken thighs, cut into bite-size pieces

1 tsp salt

FOR THE CURRY

¾ cup / 165g ghee   ↔ unsalted butter

1 large onion, finely chopped

1 star anise   ⁓ optional

1 cinnamon stick   ⁓ optional

3 to 4 cloves   ⁓ optional

½ tsp cumin seeds

1 tsp ground cumin

1 tsp garam masala

1 tsp ground coriander

2 tsp chili powder

1 tsp salt   ↔ to taste

3 Tbsp tomato paste

1 x 14-oz / 400g can of diced tomatoes

1 cup / 240ml heavy cream

2 Tbsp dried fenugreek   ⁓ optional
leaves (kasoori methi)

juice of ½ a lemon

a small handful of fresh cilantro

Preheat the broiler to the highest setting.

Bash the garlic, ginger, and chiles in a pestle and mortar to form a paste. Alternatively, finely chop or blitz in a food processor. In a large bowl mix all the marinade ingredients, then stir in half the garlic paste. Add the chicken and mix well. If you are making this ahead you can now cover and leave in the fridge until the next day. If not, carry on as below.

Place the marinated chicken on a baking sheet and broil until it's charred, 5 to 6 minutes per side. (It doesn't need to cook through at this stage.)

In a large pan melt the butter over medium heat. Once it's melted, add the onion, star anise, cinnamon stick, and cloves, if using, and the cumin seeds. Cook for about 10 minutes until the onions turn golden and caramelized. Add the remaining garlic paste, the ground spices, salt, and tomato paste. Cook for another 10 minutes until the tomato paste separates from the oil.

Add the diced tomatoes and cook for 15 to 20 minutes until the sauce thickens and the oil separates from the tomato mixture creating a rich sauce.

Add the chicken along with any accumulated juices. Stir in the cream and fenugreek leaves, if using. Stir well and cook for about 5 minutes until the chicken is fully cooked through.

Squeeze in the lemon juice, taste, and adjust the seasoning if necessary.

Garnish with cilantro and serve with rice and naan bread.

NOTE

→ *Don't stress about the whole spices – they're optional. If you've got them, toss 'em in. But there's no need to make a special trip to the store. What's important, though, is to use good-quality chili powder from the international foods aisle at your local supermarket. It really makes a difference!*

VARIATION – MAKE IT VEGGIE

→ *Replace the chicken with 1 lb / 450g of paneer or tofu tossed with ⅓ cup / 45g cornstarch. Omit the yogurt and toss the tofu or paneer with the same spices as the chicken until well coated, then pan-fry it until deliciously golden. Add it to the dish at the same point you would the chicken.*

SERVING IDEA

→ *Serve this with buttered naan, a side of rice, and some sliced red onions tossed in lemon juice and salt.*

LEFTOVERS

→ *Make a quick little butter chicken grilled cheese by layering cheese, green chutney (page 165), and leftover curry between two slices of bread and toasting until golden.*

SPECIAL

161

ALL I WANT IS SOMETHING …

CURRIED CABBAGE WEDGES

Cabbage is one of the most versatile and scrumptious vegetables you can find. It offers a savory, slightly sweet taste and is so moreish. This fall-apart braised cabbage is incredibly simple to make, and is a mix of Thai yellow curry and Indian tarka (where spices and curry leaves are tempered in oil and poured over the top), resulting in a fantastic flavor combination. Don't forget the crispy, garlicky tarka – it's a must-have, and if you can get your hands on some curry leaves, even better. Be sure to serve this with a generous bowl of rice for soaking up all those delicious oils.

1 medium head of green cabbage, quartered

1 lemongrass stalk

4 green chiles, stemmed

3 shallots, peeled ↔ 1 large onion

1½ inches / 4cm ginger

3 garlic cloves, peeled

½ tsp ground turmeric

3 Tbsp unrefined coconut oil

1 x 14-oz / 400ml can of coconut milk

1 lime, halved

salt

FOR THE TARKA

4 Tbsp unrefined coconut oil

6 cloves of garlic, thinly sliced

1 tsp cumin seeds

½ tsp ground turmeric

a few sprigs of curry leaves, leaves picked

Put the cabbage quarters into a bowl and sprinkle them with ½ tsp of salt.

Heat an ovenproof skillet and drizzle with 1 Tbsp of the coconut oil. Sear the cabbage wedges on all the cut sides until they turn golden brown. Set aside.

Preheat the oven to 400°F / 200°C.

Bash the lemongrass with the handle of a knife to separate the fibers, then finely chop. Blitz the chiles, shallots, ginger, garlic, turmeric, and lemongrass in a mini food processor.

Heat the remaining 2 Tbsp coconut oil in a cast-iron frying pan the same pan the cabbage is in, and fry the chile-shallot mixture for 5 minutes until it softens. Add the coconut milk and 1 tsp of salt. Bring to a boil, then pour over the cabbage wedges in the skillet. Bake in the oven for 30 minutes or until tender.

When the cabbage is almost ready, prepare the tarka. Heat the coconut oil in a small pan over high heat and add the garlic, cumin seeds, and turmeric. Cook for 3 minutes, or until the garlic starts to turn brown around the edges. Add the curry leaves and cook for 30 seconds.

Once the cabbage is cooked, use a spoon to drizzle on the tarka.

Squeeze the lime over the cabbage and serve on a bed of rice.

NOTES
→ To speed up the process, consider using store-bought yellow Thai curry paste instead of the fresh spices.

→ Unfortunately, there is no direct substitute for curry leaves. If you can't find them, it's best just to leave them out. However, I would recommend grabbing some whenever you come across them and storing them in the freezer.

ALL I WANT IS SOMETHING …

SEEMA'S FRIED CHICKEN

If I were the Colonel, this is what a family bucket would look like: crispy, golden crust enveloping succulent tandoori chicken, all dusted with my (not-so-secret) special spice blend. When it comes to fried foods, I'm a firm believer in adding spice dust: it allows you to infuse incredible flavors without loading up the batter or flour. In fact, you can keep this spice blend handy in a jar and sprinkle it over just about anything.

FOR THE SECRET SPICE MIX

1 Tbsp chili powder

1 Tbsp ground cumin

1 Tbsp garlic powder

1 tsp garam masala

½ tsp black pepper

2 Tbsp sugar

1 Tbsp MSG

1 Tbsp salt

FOR THE CHICKEN

2 eggs

¾ cup / 180g plain full-fat yogurt

juice of 1 lemon

1 tsp chili powder

4 cloves of garlic, grated

1½ inches / 4cm ginger, grated

4½ lb / 2kg skin-on chicken drumsticks and thighs

1 Tbsp spice mix

2¼ cups / 315g all-purpose flour

salt

FOR THE MASALA GRAVY

¼ cup / 55g unsalted butter

1 onion, finely chopped

2 Tbsp spice mix

¼ cup / 35g all-purpose flour

2½ cups / 600ml chicken stock

FOR DEEP-FRYING

2 qt / 1.9L vegetable oil or enough for deep-frying

FOR THE GREEN CHUTNEY

a large handful of fresh cilantro

a small handful of fresh mint

2 green chiles, stemmed

½ cup / 60g roasted peanuts ~ optional

juice of 1 lemon

½ cup / 120g plain full-fat yogurt

SPECIAL

165

ALL I WANT IS SOMETHING . . .

Combine all the ingredients for the secret spice mix in a bowl and adjust to your taste preferences (more chili, more garlic, etc.).

Combine the eggs, yogurt, lemon juice, chili powder, garlic, and ginger in a large bowl and add the chicken pieces and 1 Tbsp of the spice mix. Set aside to marinate for 30 minutes. (If you want to prep a day ahead, you can cover and transfer to the fridge overnight.)

For the masala gravy, add the butter to a small saucepan and gently cook the onions for 12 to 18 minutes until softened and caramelized. Add 2 Tbsp of the spice mix, cook for 30 seconds, then add the ¼ cup flour. Whisk well and gradually add the chicken stock to make a thick gravy. Bring to a boil, then remove from the heat and season to taste; keep warm.

In a large pot or Dutch oven, heat the vegetable oil to 350°F / 175°C.

Add the 2¼ cups flour to a shallow dish and season with salt. Dip the chicken pieces into the flour, pressing and squeezing to coat the chicken thoroughly. Repeat the process three times to create a craggy texture – this is the trick to making the chicken extra crispy!

Deep-fry the chicken pieces in batches for 10 to 20 minutes until they are golden and very crispy. Use a thermometer to check the internal temperature at the thickest part – it should be 165°F / 75°C.

Drain the fried chicken on paper towels and sprinkle generously with more spice mix.

While the chicken is frying, make the green chutney by blending the cilantro, mint, chiles, peanuts, if using, lemon juice, and yogurt together in a blender until smooth.

Serve the fried chicken with the gravy and green chutney.

NOTES

→　While you can experiment with different spice combinations, make sure you keep the sugar, salt, and MSG in the mix. This unique blend of seasonings is the secret to making fried chicken truly finger-licking good!

→　Plan on serving approximately one drumstick and one thigh per person. If you prefer boneless chicken, remember to reduce the frying time by half.

SPECIAL

ALL I WANT IS SOMETHING …

CRISPY CHILE-GARLIC KERALA SHRIMP

Kerala has some of the most delicious fish and shellfish I've ever had, smothered in garlic and fried in coconut oil. I've been dreaming of it ever since. Seafood with Indian flavors isn't something that I grew up with, but it is incredibly popular in the south of India. Make sure you mop up that crispy garlic chile oil with some hot rice or naan. I know you're not supposed to have favorites, but this may be my favorite recipe in the book!

2½ lb / 1.1kg head-on, shell-on shrimp

6 Tbsp / 100ml unrefined coconut oil

1 head of garlic, cloves peeled and roughly chopped

4 Tbsp unsweetened shredded coconut

10 long dried chiles (e.g. Sichuan chiles, De arbol chiles, but *definitely not* Thai chiles), stemmed and finely chopped

1 Tbsp red pepper flakes (plus an extra Tbsp if you like)

1 Tbsp chili powder, see note

3 Tbsp crispy shallots or onions

½ tsp sugar

½ tsp MSG

10 fresh curry leaves

2 limes, cut into wedges

1 tsp salt

Shell and devein the shrimp, keeping the heads on – they add lots of flavor to the oil and are great to suck on.

In a large skillet, melt the coconut oil and add the garlic and shredded coconut. Cook for 5 minutes over medium heat until the garlic is golden brown and crispy. Decrease the heat to low and add the chiles, red pepper flakes, chili powder, if using, shallots, sugar, salt, and MSG. Cook for another 2 minutes until the oils start to look red.

Add the shrimp to the pan and cook for 2 minutes per side. Before flipping them over, add the curry leaves and a splash of water.

Toss the shrimp well in the garlic and lay them out on a platter. Add some wedges of lime and enjoy with rice or hot naan.

NOTE

→ *Dried chiles and red pepper flakes vary a lot in heat, so try your chile oil and add a bit more chili powder if you want it spicier. In this recipe I use Sichuan long dried chiles, which tend not to be too spicy. And if you want to reduce the heat, remove the seeds!*

ALL I WANT IS SOMETHING …

SIZZLING BROWN BUTTER TANDOORI LAMB CHOPS

Every Christmas everyone waits for my cousin Mitesh's famous lamb chops. They are incredibly tender and tossed in a chile-garlic brown butter. I look forward to them every year, and I hope you enjoy them as much as I do. To make this a real feast, serve the lamb with my Indian-style tahdig with onion and peas, and of course a sour vinegary mint chutney (see page 172).

1 head of garlic

8 green finger chiles, stemmed

2 inches / 5cm ginger

¼ cup / 60g plain full-fat yogurt

2 lemons

½ tsp amchoor   ↔ sumac or lime zest
(unripe mango) powder

1 tsp ground cumin

1 tsp garam masala

1 tsp dried fenugreek   ⁓ optional

2 tsp chili powder

½ tsp black pepper

1 x 2½ lb / 1.1kg lamb rack, cut into chops

¼ cup / 55g unsalted butter

2 onions, thinly sliced

2 Tbsp vegetable oil

Preheat the oven to 425°F / 220°C.

Remove 3 cloves of garlic from the head, peel, and pound them together in a mortar and pestle with 4 of the chiles and the ginger.

Keep the remaining cloves of garlic in their skins; halve the remaining 4 chiles lengthwise.

Combine the pounded garlic mixture in a bowl with the yogurt, the juice of 1 of the lemons, the amchoor, and ground spices. Add the lamb chops and marinate for 30 minutes or overnight.

Remove the lamb chops from the marinade, place on a baking sheet, and roast for 8 minutes, or until they're a few minutes away from being cooked.

Meanwhile, heat the butter and oil in a skillet. Add the lamb chops, unpeeled garlic cloves, and halved chiles. Fry for 2 to 3 minutes per side over high heat until the lamb is dark and caramelized.

Transfer the lamb to a plate to rest and toss the onions into the buttery pan. Cook for 5 minutes until charred and softened.

Put the lamb chops on top of the onions and serve sizzling. Squeeze lemon juice on top.

NOTE

→   *Toss some rice in the pan with the lamb juices for a great chef's treat! Also note that this lamb is cooked medium rare – if you prefer it rare, reduce the roasting time to 5 minutes.*

ALL I WANT IS SOMETHING ...

CRISPY CUMIN RICE & PEAS (TAHDIG STYLE)

2 cups / 400g basmati rice

2 onions, chopped

1 tsp cumin seeds

2 Tbsp plain full-fat yogurt

¾ cup / 100g frozen peas

vegetable oil

salt

Wash the rice three times until the water runs almost clear, then let it soak in cold water for 30 minutes.

Bring a large pot of heavily salted water to a boil and add the rice. Cook for 5 minutes until par-cooked, then drain.

Meanwhile, cook the onions and cumin seeds in a skillet over medium-high heat with a glug of oil for 10 minutes.

In a bowl combine 1 cup of rice with the yogurt. Press this into the bottom of a nonstick lidded pot.

Combine the remaining rice with the onions and peas and spread on top of the yogurt rice.

Wrap a kitchen towel around the lid of the pot and place the lid on securely. Cook over medium-low heat for 25 to 30 minutes, until you can start to see the rice around the edges turning crispy.

Remove the lid and (very dramatically) flip the rice onto a plate. Tap very firmly on the base of the pan to release the crispy rice.

If your rice doesn't come off in one piece, scrape it off with a spatula and arrange on a plate – it will taste just as good!

VINEGARY MINT CHUTNEY

a large handful of fresh mint

¼ cup / 60ml olive oil

2 Tbsp apple cider vinegar

1 green chile, stemmed and chopped

½ tsp salt

Using a food processor, blend all the ingredients together and serve.

CARAMELIZED ORANGE SICHUAN BRAISED OXTAIL

When it comes to braising meat, oxtail is the underdog. It's a relatively cheap cut, packed with so much flavor, and the marrow in the middle melts into the sauce to create something really magical. I've used my favorite Jamaican oxtail stew, creating a base of dark caramel and then enriching it with Sichuan flavors and spices for a deeply rich dish. The only way to finish this off is by gnawing on the bones at the end – don't worry, no one's watching!

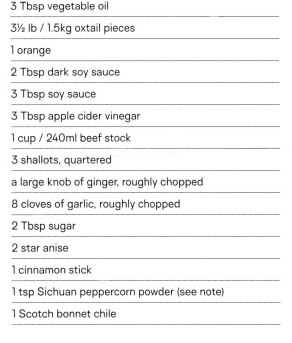

3 Tbsp vegetable oil

3½ lb / 1.5kg oxtail pieces

1 orange

2 Tbsp dark soy sauce

3 Tbsp soy sauce

3 Tbsp apple cider vinegar

1 cup / 240ml beef stock

3 shallots, quartered

a large knob of ginger, roughly chopped

8 cloves of garlic, roughly chopped

2 Tbsp sugar

2 star anise

1 cinnamon stick

1 tsp Sichuan peppercorn powder (see note)

1 Scotch bonnet chile

Heat the oil in a heavy pot over high heat. Add the oxtail pieces and brown them for 2 minutes on all sides until they are deeply golden. Transfer to a plate.

Using a knife, cut the peel off the orange and set aside. Squeeze the orange juice into a liquid measuring cup and add the dark soy, light soy, vinegar, and beef stock.

Add the shallots, ginger, garlic, and sugar to the pot you browned the oxtail in. Allow to caramelize over medium heat and brown for 5 minutes so the sugar melts and turns amber.

Deglaze the pot with the orange juice mixture and return the oxtail to the pot along with the orange peel, star anise, cinnamon stick, and Sichuan peppercorn powder. Poke holes in the Scotch bonnet with a knife, leaving it whole, and add it to the pot.

Bring to a boil, then decrease the heat to low and simmer for 3 hours, covered with the lid slightly ajar, or until the meat is falling-off-the-bone tender.

Remove the Scotch bonnet and serve over egg-fried rice (recipe opposite) to soak up all of that delicious sauce.

NOTES

→   If you are looking for something a bit more meaty, just replace the oxtail with bone-in short ribs. Try to use something on the bone for more flavor.

→   If you only have whole Sichuan peppercorns, crush them in a mortar and pestle.

ALL I WANT IS SOMETHING . . .

SPECIAL

EGG-FRIED RICE

When it comes to fried rice, simplicity is best (this is also a fantastic way to use up leftover rice in the fridge).

3 cloves of garlic, roughly chopped

2 cups / 300g leftover rice

2 eggs

1 Tbsp soy sauce

2 green onions, roughly chopped

vegetable oil

½ tsp salt

Heat up a large glug of oil in a wok over medium-high heat (pour the oil around the edge of the wok so it falls to the center and is evenly spread out).

Increase the heat to high and add the garlic. Cook for 30 seconds until fragrant, then add the rice. Break up the rice with the back of a spoon and toss with the garlic.

Push the rice to one side and crack in the eggs. Break up the eggs and cook separately from the rice until they are scrambled.

Combine the eggs with the rice. Add the soy sauce, salt, and green onions and toss well.

SPECIAL

ALL I WANT IS SOMETHING …

SPICED CHIPOTLE SHORT RIB RAGÙ

Here, soft and buttery short ribs are simmered with smoky chipotle chiles to make one of my all-time favorite slow-cooked pasta sauces. All the spiciness and warmth of chipotle braised beef tossed through with red wine and pappardelle. Every time I make this my apartment smells like the most delicious, warming stew you can imagine. It's hearty and spicy and you will certainly need some soft bread to mop up every last bit left in the bottom of the bowl.

1 x 16-oz / 450g jar of roasted red peppers, drained

2½ lb / 1.1kg boneless beef short ribs

1 tsp cumin seeds

1 tsp coriander seeds

1 tsp red pepper flakes

5 oz / 140g pancetta,   ↔ bacon
finely chopped

1 onion, finely chopped

2 celery stalks, finely chopped

1 carrot, finely chopped

6 cloves of garlic, thinly sliced

¼ cup / 60g minced   ↔ dried chipotles
canned chipotle chile in   (see notes)
adobo sauce

1 cup / 240ml dry red wine

1 x 14-oz / 400g can of diced tomatoes

1 tsp dried oregano

1½ lb / 680g pappardelle

2 oz / 55g Pecorino, grated (about 1 cup), for serving

a small handful of fresh parsley, finely chopped, for serving

olive oil

salt

Finely chop half the red peppers and blitz up the rest with an immersion blender.

Heat a large glug of oil in a heavy pot over high heat. Salt the short ribs liberally and sear on all sides until very golden. Put on a plate and set aside.

Add 1 Tbsp of oil to the pot and decrease the heat to medium. Add the cumin seeds, coriander seeds, red pepper flakes, pancetta, onion, celery, carrot, and garlic and fry for 15 minutes until caramelized and golden.

Add the chipotles and fry for 3 minutes until darkened slightly. Deglaze the pot with the wine. Add the chopped peppers, blended peppers, tomatoes, and oregano, and bring to a boil, and add the beef. Cover and simmer for 3 to 4 hours or until the meat is fork-tender and falling apart.

Remove the beef from the pot and shred with a fork. Put it back into the sauce and add 1 tsp of salt.

Cook the pasta until al dente according to the package instructions and drain, reserving the cooking water. Add the pasta to the pot of meat sauce and combine well, adding some of the pasta water to make a thick, glossy sauce.

Serve with the grated Pecorino and chopped parsley.

NOTES

→   *Substitute braising beef such as chuck for a cheaper alternative. You can also use lamb shoulder.*

→   *To make your own roasted red peppers, preheat the broiler to the highest setting. Rub whole red bell peppers with oil and pop them under the broiler for 15 minutes or until the skin is charred – you can also do this on a gas burner or using a blowtorch. Once charred, put the peppers in a bowl with a plate on top and let steam for 15 minutes, then peel.*

→   *To use dried chipotles, soak 5 chipotle chiles in ⅔ cup / 160ml of boiling water for 10 minutes, then blitz up.*

SPICY THAI-STYLE PORCHETTA

If you're looking for a main that's going to please almost everyone, this is it. Everybody gets a bit of the best parts – the crackling skin and the juicy, spicy pork. It's packed full of flavor and is incredibly impressive. Dipped in a Thai-style nam jim jaew dipping sauce, which is wonderfully sour and spicy, perfect with the fatty pork belly, and served with lots of rice – try subbing this for your Sunday dinner. The trickiest part is the tying-up, but if you know how to tie your shoelaces, you can truss a pork belly.

1 large boneless pork belly
(ask the butcher to take the ribs off)

2 shallots, roughly chopped

1 head of garlic, cloves roughly chopped

a small handful of Thai basil ↔ regular basil

6 Thai red chiles, stemmed and roughly chopped

1½ inches / 4cm ginger, roughly chopped

1 lemongrass stalk, roughly chopped

6 makrut lime leaves

1 tsp salt

FOR THE CRISPY SKIN MIX

1 Tbsp salt

½ tsp sugar

½ tsp MSG

2 tsp baking powder

FOR THE NAM JIM JAEW

2 Tbsp jasmine rice ↔ any rice

a small handful of fresh cilantro, chopped

1 small shallot, finely sliced

6 Tbsp / 90ml fish sauce

juice of 2 limes

1 tsp brown sugar

1 tsp red pepper flakes

TO SERVE

Thai basil ↔ Italian basil

baby gem lettuce

SPECIAL

ALL I WANT IS SOMETHING …

Lay the pork belly flat on the work surface skin-side up and slice parallel to the work surface across its width, just below the top layer of skin, until almost, but not quite, through to the other side. Open the pork belly up like a book so that the skin is now facing down. Very gently crosshatch the meat side of the belly, being careful not to cut all the way through.

Blitz the shallots, garlic, basil, chiles, ginger, lemongrass, and lime leaves in a food processor to form a paste. Season with 1 tsp of salt. Spread this all over the entire top side of the pork (both the meat side of the pork belly and the underside of the skin layer), massaging it into the crevices made by the crosshatching.

Using kitchen twine, roll the meat up and tie tightly so that the knot is at the top. Repeat at 1½-inch / 4cm intervals until you have a tightly tied roast.

Combine the salt, sugar, MSG, and baking powder in a small bowl and liberally coat the skin of the pork. Put the meat into the fridge for at least 4 hours or ideally overnight (the longer it sits the more chance you have of crispy skin).

When you're ready to cook, preheat the oven to 300°F / 150°C. Place the pork on a wire rack set in a rimmed baking sheet and roast in the center of the oven for 1½ to 2½ hours, depending on the size. After 1½ hours, check the temperature by inserting a thermometer in the thickest part, repeating every 30 minutes until it reaches 150°F / 65°C.

Increase the oven to 475°F / 245°C and roast for 15 to 30 minutes until the skin is puffed up and crisp, making sure to keep an eye on it. Let rest for 15 minutes before slicing.

For the nam jim jaew, toast the rice in a small skillet until golden then crush to a fine powder in a mortar and pestle. Put the cilantro and shallots into a bowl and mix with the rice powder, fish sauce, lime juice, brown sugar, and red pepper flakes. Add ¼ cup / 60ml of hot water to dissolve the sugar and mix well.

Slice the porchetta and serve with Thai basil leaves, baby gem lettuce, and the nam jim jaew.

LEFTOVERS

→ *When I've had leftovers I've finely chopped the meat, fried it, and had it in tacos with some salsa!*

SPECIAL

ALL I WANT IS SOMETHING …

STICKY TAMARIND COLA RIBS

If you bought your pork belly for the porchetta recipe from a butcher, you may have also picked up pork ribs. So this recipe is to pair with the porchetta, but is also fantastic if you just want some seriously simple sticky ribs.

2½ lb / 1.1kg pork ribs (St. Louis-style spare ribs or baby back ribs), rack cut into 6-inch / 15cm sections

1½ inches / 4cm ginger, grated

6 cloves of garlic, grated

1 cup / 240ml cola

2 Tbsp tamarind paste

3 Tbsp soy sauce

1 Tbsp sugar

½ tsp fennel seeds ⎯ optional

2 star anise

1 cinnamon stick

Preheat the oven to 300°F / 150°C; place all the ribs in a roasting pan so they lie flat and snug.

Put the ginger and garlic into a small pan and add the cola, tamarind paste, soy sauce, sugar, fennel seeds, if using, star anise, and cinnamon stick. Bring to a boil over high heat and cook until reduced by half.

Pour the cola mixture over the ribs and roast for 2 hours until they are extremely tender and sticky.

SPECIAL

NOTES

→ *This marinade works great with chicken wings too!*

→ *The cola must be regular, not diet, so you get the sugar to caramelize in the oven!*

ALL I WANT IS SOMETHING …

SPICY & SOUR PORK BELLY RICE

One of my kitchen indulgences is fatty, buttery rice (as seen in my gochujang steak recipe, see page 188). When rice absorbs rich, luscious fats it becomes soft, tender, and irresistibly juicy. This is what I dream about. In this recipe the pork belly fat is cooked out and soaked up by the rice, then it's all coated with a spicy, sour sauce inspired by the Sri Lankan black pork curry.

1 lb / 450g skin-on pork belly, cut into bite-size pieces

1 tsp sugar

2 Tbsp soy sauce

2 Tbsp balsamic vinegar

2 Tbsp tamarind paste

3 large onions, thinly sliced

1 lemongrass stalk

6 cloves of garlic, peeled

1¼ inches / 3cm ginger

6 green chiles, stemmed

15 curry leaves

1 tsp cumin seeds

1 tsp chili powder

1 tsp garam masala

1 Tbsp tomato paste

vegetable oil

salt

FOR THE RICE

2 cups / 400g basmati rice

2 lemons, thinly sliced

a small handful of fresh cilantro, finely chopped

1 large pinch of saffron   ↔ turmeric

3 Tbsp milk, warmed

NOTE
→   Replace the pork belly with chicken, lamb, or beef. Reduce the cooking time to 30 minutes if using chicken.

Put the pork belly pieces into a bowl and toss with the sugar, soy sauce, vinegar, and tamarind paste.

Cook the onions with ¼ cup / 60ml of oil and a pinch of salt in a heavy pot or Dutch oven over medium-high heat for 10 to 15 minutes or until crispy. Use a fine-mesh sieve to drain the onions, reserving the oil. Use the back of a knife to bash the lemongrass, starting at the tip, then finely chop and blitz in the food processor with the garlic, ginger, and chiles.

Put 2 Tbsp of the reserved onion oil back into the pot and add the curry leaves, cumin seeds, and garlic mixture. Cook for 5 minutes over medium heat then add the chili powder, garam masala, and tomato paste.

Cook for 5 minutes, until the tomato paste has darkened, then add ¾ cup / 175ml of water and mix well. Add the pork belly with its marinade, three-quarters of the crispy onions, and 1 tsp of salt. Mix well and bring to a boil.

Decrease the heat to low and simmer, partially covered, for 2 hours. (The pork should be buttery soft and fork-tender with a thick sauce.) Skim 3 Tbsp of fat off the top, or more, depending on how fatty the meat was. Taste and adjust the seasoning, adding more tamarind if you want it more sour.

Meanwhile, wash the rice three times until the water runs almost clear, then let it soak in cold water for 30 minutes.

Once the pork is almost done, bring a large pan of heavily salted water to a boil and add the rice. Cook for 5 minutes then drain – you are only parcooking the rice.

Rub the bottom of a large, heavy pot with oil and layer in half the rice. Layer in the pork belly and half the lemon slices, then top with the remaining rice, lemon slices, the cilantro, remaining crispy onions, and pork fat. Grind the saffron and let steep in the milk for 5 minutes, then sprinkle the saffron milk over the rice. Wrap the lid of the pot with a kitchen towel and cover the rice.

Place the pot over medium heat. When you begin to see steam, decrease the heat to low and cook for 20 minutes.

Turn the heat off and let sit for 10 minutes before serving.

SPECIAL

ALL I WANT IS SOMETHING...

GOCHUJANG BUTTER STEAK

I'm not really a big steak or beef eater so when I do have it, I want it to be very special. While fries are great, and are the classic pairing for steak, I don't think they really cut it – are they going to soak up all those delicious steak juices and butter? No, I don't think so, and this is why I think we should all be eating our steaks with rice. Once you try it I know you will be convinced. My spicy umami gochujang butter and steak juices perfectly smother the short-grain rice for a really special steak dinner (you can even have some fries on the side if you really must!).

2 x 8-oz / 225g boneless rib-eye steaks, about ¾ inch / 2cm thick

1 cup / 200g short-grain rice

2 cloves of garlic, unpeeled

1 Tbsp unsalted butter

vegetable oil

salt

FOR THE GOCHUJANG BUTTER

¼ cup / 55g unsalted butter, softened

1 Tbsp gochujang

2 Tbsp finely chopped fresh cilantro

1 clove of garlic, grated

1 Tbsp soy sauce

½ tsp chili crisp

½ tsp honey

a pinch of flaky sea salt

Heavily salt the steaks and let them sit for about 30 minutes at room temperature or in the fridge overnight. If you don't have at least 30 minutes, just salt them right before cooking.

Rinse the rice in cold water three times, until the water is almost clear. Alternatively, soak the rice for 30 minutes.

Drain the rice and put into a pan with 1¼ cups / 300ml of water. Bring to a boil, then decrease the heat to low and cook, covered, for 12 minutes. Turn off the heat and let sit for 10 minutes with the lid on.

Beat the ingredients for the gochujang butter in a bowl. Lay out a large piece of plastic wrap and spoon the butter into the middle. Roll up the plastic wrap to form a butter log and twist the ends. Place in the freezer for 10 minutes to firm up slightly (you don't want it to freeze). Or, if you're feeling cheffy, you could also try quenelling the butter for an extra fancy finish.

Crush the garlic, keeping the skins on.

Heat a few Tbsp of oil in a cast-iron skillet on the highest heat until smoking. Add the steaks and cook for 3 minutes on one side (this will be roughly 4 minutes in total for rare, 5 to 6 minutes in total for medium and 8 to 10 minutes for well done). Once you have flipped the steaks once and they're nicely seared on both sides add the butter and crushed garlic cloves. Baste the steaks with the butter for 2 minutes.

Remove the steaks from the pan and let rest for 5 minutes. Slice against the grain and serve on top of the rice. Top with a slice of gochujang butter and allow it to melt slightly, then drizzle with any remaining meat juices.

LEFTOVERS
→ *If you have extra gochujang butter store it in the fridge and use it to cook up some eggs or to slather over a grilled cheese!*

ALL I WANT IS SOMETHING …

ALL I WANT IS ...

SOMETHING SWEET

THE BROWNIE RECIPE

This may be my most prized recipe, and I am gifting it to you in my book. When I so tragically got fired from my job in the midst of Covid, my friend convinced me to start selling brownies to make some money. I spent months developing the recipe, trying every brownie hack I've ever come across on the internet, getting feedback from Google Forms to make them better, even getting boxes designed so I could ship them across the country. We were selling hundreds of boxes a week, all being sold out in a matter of minutes and made by me and my mum in our tiny kitchen in Slough. I don't think I'll be selling them again any time soon, so for now you can use this recipe to make them at home.

8 oz / 225g dark chocolate

1 cup / 200g light brown sugar   ↔ dark brown sugar

14 Tbsp / 200g unsalted butter, softened

½ cup / 70g all-purpose flour

⅓ cup / 45g cornstarch

⅓ cup / 30g cocoa powder

1 tsp baking powder

½ tsp salt

2 oz / 55g white chocolate

4 eggs

Preheat the oven to 325°F / 165°C, and line an 8-inch / 20cm square baking pan with parchment paper.

Melt 6 oz / 170g of the dark chocolate in the microwave at 50% power, 30 seconds at a time, stirring in between.

Beat the sugar and butter in a stand mixer fitted with the paddle attachment until pale and fluffy, 3 to 5 minutes.

Meanwhile, sift together the flour, cornstarch, cocoa powder, baking powder, and salt.

Roughly chop the remaining dark chocolate and the white chocolate into irregular-sized chunks.

Add the eggs to the sugar and butter one by one, mixing well after each addition. (Don't worry if the batter looks curdled at this point; it will smooth out once you add the dry ingredients.)

Once the melted chocolate has cooled slightly add it to the batter, drizzling it in a stream down the side of the bowl with the mixer running.

Add the flour mixture and mix until just combined, then stir in three-quarters of the chopped white and dark chocolate.

Pour the batter into the prepared pan, smooth into an even layer with a spatula, and sprinkle with the remaining chopped chocolate.

Bake for 15 minutes, then remove from the oven and tap firmly against the countertop. Let sit for 15 minutes. Bake again for 20 to 25 minutes – it will still be very soft and have a light jiggle. A toothpick should come out with moist crumbs, neither totally sticky nor clean. Careful not to hit a melted chocolate puddle (I would insert two toothpicks at different points to be certain!).

Let cool completely, then refrigerate for at least 4 hours to set.

Slice into squares and serve.

NOTE

→   *These are cooked quite low and slow to make them extra fudgy. I also found leaving them out for 15 minutes mid-bake creates the most delicious melt-in-your-mouth texture.*

SWEET

ALL I WANT IS SOMETHING …

DOUGHNUTS TWO WAYS

There really is nothing like a homemade doughnut. Trust me, when you make them at home and realize how easy they are you'll put every single bakery doughnut to shame. They really do taste the best within three hours of frying, so keep that in mind.

I've given you two filling options here, both equally easy.

First up, a game-changing hack – melting down a high-quality pistachio ice cream. Why start from scratch when someone has already done the hard work for you? Pistachio butter is a pain to find, and don't even get me started on making your own. Let the ice cream do the heavy lifting and enjoy the pistachio bliss.

The second is as if a custard doughnut and a sour gummy candy had a baby. I had this idea because the sugary lips you get from traditional doughnuts reminded me of the same feeling you get from sour gummy candies like Sour Patch Kids and Tangfastics. It's sweet but sour, creamy, and it balances all the richness from the doughnut.

SWEET

FOR THE DOUGH

⅔ cup / 160ml whole milk

2 Tbsp sugar

2¼ tsp instant or rapid-rise yeast

1¾ cups / 245g bread flour, plus more for dusting

¼ tsp salt

1 egg, beaten

¼ cup / 55g unsalted butter, softened and cut into 8 pieces

vegetable oil

FOR THE PISTACHIO ICE CREAM FILLING

1 pint / 475ml pistachio ice cream

¼ cup / 35g cornstarch

1 Tbsp pistachio paste   ⸺ optional

¾ cup / 175ml heavy cream

3 Tbsp sugar

FOR THE TANGFASTIC FILLING

1 cup / 240ml heavy cream

4 Tbsp / 50g sugar

1 cup / 325g strawberry   ↔ your favorite jam
or raspberry jam

1½ tsp citric acid

NOTES

→   Don't worry too much if your ice cream pint isn't exactly 475ml – anywhere between 450ml and 500ml will do!

→   If you can get ahold of it, try using pistachio kulfi instead of traditional ice cream.

→   Fill the doughnuts when you are ready to serve. They will stay fresh in an airtight container for 1 day, but they are best filled and eaten on the same day as they're fried!

ALL I WANT IS SOMETHING ...

DOUGH

Warm the milk and sugar in a saucepan until the mixture is just lukewarm – test this with your finger, it should be just warm to the touch. Stir in the yeast and let sit for 5 to 10 minutes until it starts to foam slightly. This will let you know if your yeast is still alive.

In a stand mixer fitted with a dough hook combine the flour and salt. Add the yeasty milk and the egg and mix on medium speed for 5 minutes until the dough comes away from the sides of the bowl. Cover the bowl with a clean kitchen towel or plastic wrap and let sit for 5 minutes.

With the mixer on medium–high speed add the butter 1 piece at a time until it's been absorbed into the dough. (Your butter must be soft enough to push your finger through, otherwise it won't combine with the dough.)

Knead the dough in the mixer for 8 minutes on medium speed to form a smooth, shiny dough. (It will still be very sticky.)

Cover the bowl with a kitchen towel and let the dough rise until doubled in size. This could take anywhere from 1 to 2 hours.

Punch the dough to release all the air and pull out large tangerine-size balls (about 2 oz / 55g). Flatten each ball on a lightly floured work surface and fold the outsides into the middle. Turn the ball over and roll it into a smooth ball with your hands.

Cut out eight 4-inch / 10cm squares of parchment paper. Transfer the dough balls to a baking sheet, putting each ball on a square of parchment. Cover with plastic wrap and let rise until doubled in size; this should take 30 to 60 minutes. When fully risen they will spring back halfway when you gently press the side with your index finger.

Meanwhile, heat 1½ inches / 4cm of oil in a large pot until it registers 325°F / 165°C.

Fry your doughnuts in the hot oil in two batches, leaving the parchment on and removing it once it's released into the oil. Cook for 2 minutes per side until golden brown. If you see a white ring (i.e. the white ring of confidence), your doughnuts will be light and airy!

Transfer to a wire rack and let cool for 20 minutes before filling.

PISTACHIO ICE CREAM FILLING

Put the ice cream into a pan and melt it down (sacrilege, I know, but it will be fine, just keep going).

Meanwhile, mix the cornstarch with ¼ cup / 60ml of water. Add to the melted ice cream and whisk together. Decrease heat to low and continue whisking for 6 to 8 minutes until the mixture is very thick and large bubbles begin to form and pop on the surface.

Whisk in the pistachio paste, if using, then transfer to a shallow bowl and place plastic wrap directly onto the surface. Refrigerate until completely chilled.

When ready to serve, whip the cream to form medium peaks. Add a large spoon of the whipped cream to the pistachio mixture and mix well with a whisk to lighten the base, then fold in the remaining whipped cream with a spatula.

Put the filling into a piping bag with a nozzle (any shape nozzle will work as long as it is big enough). Use a knife to make a hole in the side of each doughnut and pipe the filling into the hole until the doughnut feels heavy.

Coat the filled doughnuts in the sugar and serve immediately. These are best eaten the day they are made.

TANGFASTIC FILLING

Whip the cream with 1 Tbsp of the sugar until it forms stiff peaks.

Fill one piping bag with a nozzle (any shape) with the whipped cream and another with the jam.

Use a knife to make a hole in the side of each doughnut and pipe in 2 Tbsp of jam, then pipe in the whipped cream.

Combine the remaining 3 Tbsp of sugar and the citric acid in a bowl and coat the filled doughnuts. Serve immediately.

195

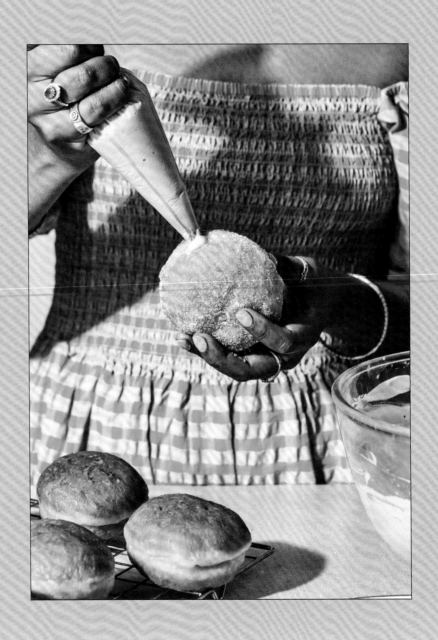

UPSIDE-DOWN RASPBERRY, ORANGE & OLIVE OIL CAKE

Upside-down cakes are one of the best baking hacks around. Carefully placing beautiful, fresh fruit at the bottom makes a glorious cake top that needs no decorating but looks incredibly impressive. Here, I've combined my favorite orange and poppy seed cake with fresh, tart raspberries.

3 cups / 360g raspberries

1¼ cups / 250g plus 3 Tbsp sugar

2 oranges, zested

1 cup / 240g thick Greek yogurt (must be full-fat)

3 large eggs

⅔ cup / 160ml extra-virgin olive oil, plus more for the pan

¼ tsp salt

1 Tbsp black poppy seeds

1½ cups / 210g all-purpose flour

½ tsp baking powder

½ tsp baking soda

Preheat the oven to 350°F / 175°C.

Grease an 8-inch / 20cm cake pan with olive oil and line the bottom with parchment paper. Gently press in the raspberries, top side down (so the hole is facing upwards), to cover the entire bottom surface of the pan. Sprinkle with 3 Tbsp of the sugar and set aside.

In a large bowl combine the remaining 1¼ cups / 250g of sugar with the orange zest and rub together with your fingers.

Add the yogurt, eggs, oil, salt, and poppy seeds and mix well.

Sift in the flour, baking powder, and baking soda and whisk to form a smooth batter.

Carefully pour the batter over the raspberries and bake for 55 to 60 minutes until a toothpick comes out clean. Let the cake cool in the pan for 20 minutes then turn out onto a cooling rack and let cool completely.

SWEET

ALL I WANT IS SOMETHING …

FUDGY BANANA BARS

I've had enough of banana bread, but I still never seem to use up all my bananas, so I developed these super-decadent bars that feel like the lovechild of fudgy brownies and banana bread. Thanks to a little cornstarch magic, a technique I learned making mochi traditionally using glutinous rice flour, the texture totally transforms as it cools. Make sure to try a piece straight out of the oven for a gooey, warm bite and then again when it's cooled for a chewy, fudgy version – both with a generous glass of cold milk!

¾ cup / 165g unsalted butter, plus more for the pan

3 small brown bananas

½ cup / 120ml sweetened condensed milk

3 eggs

1 cup / 200g dark brown sugar

¾ cup / 105g all-purpose flour, plus more for the pan

⅓ cup / 45g cornstarch

½ tsp salt

½ tsp baking powder

FOR THE FROSTING

5 oz / 140g cream cheese, softened

2 Tbsp sweetened condensed milk

1 tsp ground cinnamon

Preheat the oven to 350°F / 175°C. Butter and flour an 8-inch / 20cm square baking pan and line with parchment paper.

Melt the butter in a saucepan and cook for 15 minutes over low heat until it has browned and smells nutty. (It will start getting foamy at first, and then it will turn a nutty brown with dark solids at the bottom.) Strain the butter, reserving the dark solids for later.

Mash the bananas with the condensed milk. Use an immersion blender to make this mixture smooth if you don't want chunks of banana in your bars. Add the melted brown butter, eggs, sugar, flour, cornstarch, salt, and baking powder and whisk until smooth.

Pour into the prepared pan and bake for 30 to 35 minutes (a toothpick should come out sticky).

For the best results refrigerate for 12 hours. Try a piece straight out of the oven and then watch the texture transform over time.

For the frosting, whip the reserved brown butter solids with the cream cheese and condensed milk.

Cut the banana bars into squares and spread with the frosting. Sprinkle with a pinch of the cinnamon and enjoy.

NOTES

→   If you don't have any brown bananas and you can't wait, put your bananas into the oven for 15 minutes at 400°F / 200°C.

→   Try adding chopped nuts, chocolate, or dried fruit. You can even add spices such as cinnamon or nutmeg to the batter!

→   Save the rest of your condensed milk in an airtight container in the fridge. It will keep for weeks and is great for sweetening tea and coffee.

SWEET

ALL I WANT IS SOMETHING…

WHITE CHOCOLATE & MANDARIN BURNT BASQUE CHEESECAKE

I normally can't stand cheesecake – it always feels too heavy and stodgy. But when I tried a burnt Basque cheesecake for the first time my mind was blown. It's like a combination of a custard and a cheesecake and the inside is majorly creamy. Plus it's probably the easiest dessert you can make.

Mandarin and white chocolate hold a very special place in my heart, and it all began in a quaint ice cream shop nestled in the Isle of Wight, a place named Crave. Their best-selling ice cream was mandarin and white chocolate. It was remarkably creamy and rich, with thick Cornish cream, white chocolate, and vibrant bursts of mandarin. But the best part was Tracy and Chris, who spent their summers orchestrating wild and imaginative ice cream flavors such as mango sticky rice and lemon pancake. They would use this ice cream money to spend their winters traveling through the sunniest parts of the world, finding inspiration for their next ice cream flavor. And I think that's actually all I want in life, too.

SWEET

7 oz / 200g white chocolate, roughly chopped

1 cup / 200g plus 2 Tbsp sugar

6 clementines or mandarin oranges

2 lb / 900g cream cheese, softened

¼ tsp salt

¾ cup / 180g thick Greek yogurt

6 eggs

⅓ cup / 45g all-purpose flour

Place an oven rack in the upper-middle position and preheat the oven to 475°F / 245°C.

Lay a very large piece of parchment paper over a 9-inch / 23cm cake pan so that it covers the bottom and the sides.

Put the white chocolate into a microwave-safe bowl and melt it in the microwave at 30-second intervals, stirring in between.

Place 1 cup / 200g of the sugar in the bowl of a stand mixer and zest in 4 of the clementines. Rub the sugar and zest together until the sugar is orange – this releases the oils in the zest, making it more flavorful. Add the cream cheese, salt, and yogurt and use the paddle attachment to beat until very smooth. Add the eggs one at a time, beating after each edition.

Add the cooled white chocolate and mix. Remove about 1 cup of the batter, put it into a second bowl, and whisk in the flour until smooth. Add back to the cheesecake batter and mix until fully incorporated.

Pour the batter into the prepared pan and bake in the oven for 30 to 35 minutes. The cheesecake will be very soft and wobbly and the top will be dark, but don't worry – this is what will make it super-luscious and creamy. Let cool to room temperature on the counter, then refrigerate overnight.

Peel the 4 zested clementines, scrape off any pith, and break into segments. Juice the remaining 2 clementines. Combine the juice with the remaining 2 Tbsp of sugar and microwave for 30 seconds. Add the peeled clementine segments and mix, then pour over the cheesecake.

NOTE

→ *You can sub in any other citrus fruit you like – try grapefruit, or lemon with some lemon curd over the top.*

ALL I WANT IS SOMETHING…

CHOCOLATEY PEANUT BUTTER CARAMEL TART

This recipe honors one of my favorite candies – Reese's peanut butter cups. It's the dessert I made most often when I was at college, because all my friends raved about it, and because it tastes like a giant, luscious Reese's cupcake. The filling is a really simple peanut butter caramel, smooth and gooey, encased in a salty, savory pretzel crust.

FOR THE BASE

7 oz / 200g pretzels   ↔ graham crackers

3 Tbsp sugar

10 Tbsp / 140g unsalted butter, melted

3 Tbsp water

FOR THE PEANUT BUTTER FILLING

¾ cup / 200g crunchy peanut butter

1¼ cups / 300ml heavy cream

¾ cup / 150g light brown sugar

salt

FOR THE CHOCOLATE TOPPING

6 oz / 170g dark chocolate, broken into pieces

1 cup / 240ml heavy cream

FOR THE CRUNCHY TOPPING

2 Tbsp pretzels

2 Tbsp salted, roasted peanuts

¼ cup / 45g Reese's mini cups, chopped

a pinch of flaky sea salt

Preheat the oven to 350°F / 175°C.

In a food processor process the pretzels and sugar to a fine powder, then add the melted butter and water and pulse until the mixture resembles wet sand.

Pour half the pretzel mix into a 9-inch / 23cm deep tart pan and press it out to the edges and up the sides of the pan with your hands. Add the remaining pretzel mix and press down to make the base. Use the bottom of a measuring cup to help you press it down.

Place on a baking sheet and bake in the oven for 15 to 20 minutes.

Meanwhile, combine the peanut butter, cream, and sugar in a small saucepan and bring to a boil. Decrease the heat to low and simmer for 10 minutes, stirring and scraping the bottom of the pan constantly, until very thick. (If the oil starts to separate out and look broken at any point just whisk vigorously to re-emulsify.) If your peanut butter is unsalted, finish with a pinch of salt.

Pour the peanut caramel into the crust and let cool slightly.

Place the chocolate in a heatproof bowl. Heat the cream until steaming, pour over the chocolate, and let sit for 5 minutes. Stir until smooth, then pour over the peanut caramel layer.

For the topping, lightly crush the remaining pretzels, peanuts, Reese's mini cups, and salt and sprinkle them on top of the tart.

Chill in the fridge before serving.

NOTE

→   *Use whatever chocolate is your favorite for the topping if you like a specific brand or percentage. I love how the dark chocolate cuts through the rich filling, but if you prefer milk chocolate, use that.*

SWEET

ALL I WANT IS SOMETHING …

COCONUT CREAM KEY LIME PIE

One thing that has always had space in my brain is the coconut cream pie from that *iCarly* episode, the one where we were driven to the brink of pie-induced madness. Now, here's the thing: I never considered myself a coconut enthusiast, until I recreated it with homemade coconut cream and flakes and tasted this pie of dreams.

    This pie is a simpler but more balanced version, with a thick layer of zesty key lime – another childhood classic for me, and my brother's favorite dessert.

6 oz / 170g digestive biscuits or graham crackers

½ cup / 45g unsweetened shredded coconut, plus 2 Tbsp for topping

¾ cup / 150g plus 3 Tbsp granulated sugar

½ cup / 110g unsalted butter, melted

1 x 14-oz / 400g can of sweetened condensed milk

6 Tbsp / 90ml lime juice (from about 4 limes)

zest of 4 limes

6 Tbsp / 90g sour cream

¼ cup / 35g cornstarch

½ tsp salt

1 x 14-oz / 400ml can unsweetened coconut cream

1 cup / 240ml chilled heavy cream

Preheat the oven to 350°F / 175°C.

    In the food processor pulse the digestive biscuits with ½ cup / 45g of the shredded coconut and 3 Tbsp of the sugar to form a fine crumb.

    Add the butter and pulse until it resembles wet sand.

    Pour the mixture into a 9-inch / 23cm pie plate or fluted tart tin and press it in so it is evenly distributed up the sides and over the base. Use the bottom of a measuring cup to help you press it.

    Bake for 10 to 15 minutes until browned and fragrant, then let cool completely.

    Meanwhile, mix together the condensed milk, lime juice, lime zest, and sour cream. Pour into the tart shell and bake for 10 minutes, then remove and let cool completely.

    In a medium, heavy saucepan whisk the remaining ¾ cup / 150g of sugar with the cornstarch and salt. Whisk in the coconut cream then bring to a simmer and cook for 2 to 4 minutes until very thick, and large bubbles start to form and pop on the surface. Transfer to a bowl and press plastic wrap directly onto the surface. Refrigerate until completely chilled, at least 4 hours and up to 1 day.

    Beat the heavy cream to stiff peaks. Whisk a third of the whipped cream into the coconut mixture to lighten, then fold in the remaining whipped cream with a spatula.

    Spread the coconut cream over the chilled pie, creating texture with the back of a spoon.

    Toast the remaining 2 Tbsp of shredded coconut in a dry pan for 3 minutes until golden and sprinkle over the top of the pie.

    You can keep the pie refrigerated for a day, but add the shredded coconut when ready to serve, or serve it immediately.

SWEET

NOTE

→   *If you must, you can add a tiny drop of green food coloring to the lime layer, but be careful not to add too much so that it looks like a Shrek pie.*

ALL I WANT IS SOMETHING . . .

MASALA HOT CHOCO & CHURROS

Masala hot chocolate is a concoction I came up with in the depths of winter when my mum was making me endless cups of chai and I had so much chocolate left over from my brownie making. It's warming, lightly spiced, and so rich and creamy. Using a mix of real chocolate and cocoa powder is the trick to making it extra indulgent. And for the book I've made it into a full dessert by dunking in some crispy cinnamon churros for the perfect winter treat.

FOR THE HOT CHOCOLATE

1½ inches / 4cm ginger

5 cardamom pods

½ tsp black peppercorns

1 cinnamon stick

¾ cup / 175ml water

3 chai teabags

2½ cups / 590ml milk

3½ oz / 100g dark chocolate, chopped

1 Tbsp cocoa powder

4 Tbsp / 50g sugar, plus more as needed

½ tsp salt

FOR THE CINNAMON CHURROS

⅔ cup / 160ml milk

7 Tbsp / 100g unsalted butter

1 Tbsp sugar

1 tsp salt

1 cup / 140g all-purpose flour

3 large eggs

vegetable oil, for deep-frying

FOR THE SPICED SUGAR

¼ cup / 50g sugar

1 tsp ground cinnamon

½ tsp ground ginger

MASALA HOT CHOCO

Gently crush the whole spices and put them into a pan with the water and the opened tea bags. Boil over high heat for 10 minutes, then add the milk, decrease the heat, and simmer for another 10 minutes.

Strain the tea, discarding the spices and tea leaves, and return to the pan.

Add the chocolate, cocoa powder, sugar, and salt. Simmer for 5 minutes, whisking well, until all the chocolate has melted.

Taste, in case you want a sweeter hot chocolate, and enjoy in your favorite mug.

CINNAMON CHURROS

Heat the milk, butter, sugar, and salt in a pan over low heat until the butter is melted.

Add the flour and beat it with a wooden spoon for a few minutes until it forms a dough that pulls away from the sides of the pan.

Take it off the heat and transfer the dough to a bowl. Crack in the eggs one at a time, beating very well after each addition. The dough will be smooth and glossy.

Transfer the dough to a piping bag with a star nozzle – you can also use a ziplock bag with a hole cut out of the corner!

Mix the spiced sugar ingredients together in a small bowl.

In a large pot heat enough oil for deep-frying until 350°F / 175°C.

Pipe the churros into the hot oil, snipping off the end with scissors. Pipe 3 or 4 at a time and let them cook for a few minutes on each side until the churros are crispy and golden.

Transfer to a plate lined with paper towels and dust with the spiced sugar.

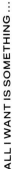

SWEET

ALL I WANT IS SOMETHING . . .

SPICED RUM STICKY TOFFEE PUDDING

Sticky toffee pudding has always been a household favorite – it's the first dessert I made successfully. I actually tested it for years, trying to get the perfect light, fluffy sponge with sweet, creamy caramel sauce that tasted like melted Werther's Originals, but was also not too sweet. There was a moment where I had to ban it because my mum was requesting it so much!

The light, fluffy sponge here has been infused with the flavors of black Jamaican rum cake. I don't often call for alcohol in my desserts, and this may be the only one I've had where the rum really complements the warmth of the spices and dark sugars.

8 oz / 225g whole medjool dates
(16 to 18 dates, weighed with pits)

3 tsp baking soda

1 tsp ground cinnamon

1 tsp grated fresh ginger

7 Tbsp / 105ml dark rum,   ↔ water
plus more for serving

6 Tbsp / 85g unsalted butter, softened

1 cup / 200g dark brown sugar

2 eggs

2 Tbsp molasses   ↔ honey

½ cup / 120ml milk

1¼ cups / 175g all-purpose flour

½ tsp salt

1 tsp baking powder

FOR THE TOFFEE SAUCE

½ cup / 110g unsalted butter, cut into pieces

1 cup / 200g dark brown sugar

1¼ cups / 300ml heavy cream

½ tsp salt

TO SERVE

vanilla ice cream

¼ cup / 55g unsalted   ⁓ optional
butter, to reheat

Preheat the oven to 350°F / 175°C. Grease a 9 by 5-inch / 23 by 13cm loaf pan and line with parchment paper.

Remove the pits from the dates, roughly chop, and add to a saucepan with ⅔ cup / 160ml of water, 1 tsp of the baking soda, the cinnamon, and ginger. Cook for 10 minutes over medium-high heat, pushing the dates down to form a thick paste. Remove from the heat and stir in the rum.

In a large bowl beat the butter and sugar until fluffy. Add the eggs, date paste, molasses, and milk and mix well. Add the flour, remaining 2 tsp of baking soda, the salt, and baking powder and mix until just combined.

Pour into the prepared pan and bake for 50 minutes until a toothpick comes out with moist crumbs.

Meanwhile, make the toffee sauce. Melt the butter in a saucepan and add the brown sugar. Cook for 10 minutes over medium-high heat, until bubbling rapidly, then add the cream. Cook for another 2 minutes and add the salt.

To serve, you can slice the cake and serve it hot with a scoop of ice cream or cream and lots of toffee sauce.

If the cake has been fully cooled, toast the slices with some butter in a pan on both sides, then top with ice cream and toffee sauce.

For some drama, pour 2 Tbsp of rum over the top of the cake and flambé with a blowtorch.

NOTES

→   I've made this in a loaf pan because I like how easy it is to serve for a big crowd, but you could make it in a 9-inch / 23cm cake pan and check it after 35 minutes of baking.

211

SWEET

ALL I WANT IS SOMETHING …

CARAMELIZED BANANA SPLIT WITH HAZELNUT CHOCOLATE FUDGE

Banana splits have recently become my favorite desserts. They look super impressive but are basically no work to make. And honestly, I feel like we often forget about them, so this is your reminder to make yourself one. A few store-bought ingredients, some sprinkles, a cherry, and you end up with a really showstopping dessert fit for anyone and everyone.

3 Tbsp heavy cream

3 Tbsp Nutella

1 banana

2 Tbsp granulated sugar

3 scoops of your favorite ice cream

canned whipped cream

2 Tbsp sprinkles

3 maraschino cherries

salt

Combine the cream and Nutella in a microwave-safe bowl and melt in the microwave for 1 minute. Stir well to create a smooth sauce. Add a pinch of salt and mix again.

Peel the banana and slice in half lengthwise. Sprinkle with the sugar and caramelize using a blowtorch. (Alternatively, place under a very hot broiler for 5 minutes until the sugar is melted and caramelized.)

Place your banana in a dish and top with the ice cream. Drizzle with the chocolate sauce and squirt some whipped cream on top. Decorate with the sprinkles and finish with the cherries.

SWEET

ALL I WANT IS SOMETHING . . .

EMERGENCY BIRTHDAY CAKE

I've always believed that any occasion can become a celebration if you have a cake. New job, passing a test, learning to ride a bike . . . this is an emergency birthday cake, but it can really be used for any occasion, and is perfect for making someone feel incredibly special for very little effort. How did you feel last time someone made you a cake?

And before the purists come for me, think of this as a combination of a Japanese fruit sando (white bread with cream and fruit in a sandwich) and a Latin American tres leches cake (a very simple cake drenched in sweetened condensed milk and topped with cream), combined with the assembly of a Swedish *smorgastorta*. It's one of my proudest creations to date and I even made it for my brother's engagement party.

FOR THE FILLING AND FROSTING

5 cups / 1.2L heavy cream

¼ cup / 30g confectioners' sugar

1 tsp vanilla extract

3 Tbsp sweetened condensed milk

¼ cup / 60ml milk

½ tsp vanilla extract

2 cups / 240g strawberries, hulled

12 slices of thick white bread (usually one loaf is enough) (see note)

6 Tbsp / 120g jam   ↪ any sweet sandwich filling (Nutella, Biscoff, marmalade)

FOR DECORATING

¼ cup / 50g sprinkles

1 tube of writing icing

Whip the cream, confectioners' sugar, and vanilla with a handheld mixer (or a regular whisk and some elbow grease) until thick and stiff enough to stand up on its own.

Combine the condensed milk, milk, and vanilla. Thinly slice the strawberries.

Cut the crusts off the bread and discard (or blitz them up and save them as breadcrumbs).

Lay out 4 slices of bread on your board or serving platter to make a base and "glue" these down with a small amount of whipped cream.

Liberally brush the bread with half the condensed milk mixture, making sure to get right to the edges.

Spread 3 Tbsp of jam on the bread, then add half the sliced strawberries and finally a thick layer of whipped cream.

Top with 4 more slices of bread and repeat with the remaining condensed milk mixture, jam, and strawberries, then finish with a layer of bread.

Cover the entire cake with whipped cream. If you like, you can pipe some of the cream in swirls on top using a piping bag. Press the sprinkles onto the side of the cake and use writing icing to add a personalized message.

NOTES

→   Use a brioche loaf for a more luxurious cake. You can even use a brioche burger bun to make a tiny lunchbox cake! Please do not use sourdough – the cheaper the white bread the better.

→   This is incredibly customizable – switch up the fruit, the jam, or use chocolate frosting if you wish. I've created a super simple base so you can enjoy the creative process!

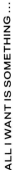
SWEET

ALL I WANT IS SOMETHING . . .

ALL I WANT IS ...

SOMETHING NOW!

EMERGENCY DUMPLING SOUP

Soups are my go-to when I'm feeling under the weather or nursing a hangover, and I always make sure to keep my freezer stocked with dumplings for cases like these. One day, after a particularly brutal hangover, I decided to combine the two, and it's been my soul-saving secret ever since. The magic ingredient is a whisked egg, which adds a delightful richness and velvetiness and just the right amount of thickness to the broth.

1 vegetable stock cube ⟷ chicken stock cube

7 to 10 frozen dumplings

1 Tbsp soy sauce

1 Tbsp Chinese black vinegar ⟷ balsamic vinegar

1 tsp chili crisp

3 green onions

1 egg

1 tsp sesame seeds ⟿ optional

Start by bringing 2 cups / 475ml of water to a simmer in a pan. Crumble in the stock cube and toss in your dumplings.

Add the soy sauce, vinegar, and chili crisp and let it all boil for 3 minutes (or according to the instructions on your dumpling package).

Meanwhile, finely chop the green onions. (For an easier option, you can use scissors and snip them directly over the soup bowl to save the hassle of getting a cutting board and knife out.)

Crack the egg into the pan and give it a good whisk to create light, feathery strands.

Pour your delicious soup into a bowl and top it with green onions and a sprinkle of sesame seeds, if you like.

NOW,

NOTE

→ *The beauty of this recipe lies in its versatility. You can toss in whatever you have lying around for extra flavor and goodness. I love adding chopped cabbage or some noodles for extra carbs. It's all about making it your own.*

ALL I WANT IS SOMETHING . . .

15-MINUTE LAKSA

The times when I don't feel like cooking are usually the times I need something warming and spicy to wake myself up. I usually have a tub of Thai curry paste in the back of the fridge, which is perfect for a really speedy laksa that tastes like you spent hours on it.

Throw in whatever green veg you like, or even some shrimp or tofu for extra protein!

2 eggs

1 to 2 Tbsp Thai red curry paste
(depending on how spicy your paste is)

1 x 14-oz / 400ml can coconut milk

1 Tbsp fish sauce   ↔ veggie fish sauce

1 Tbsp soy sauce

½ tsp sugar

8 oz / 225g instant ramen noodles (two packs)

any green veg (bok choy, sugar snap peas,
asparagus, spinach)

vegetable oil

TO SERVE

green onions, chopped

Bring a pan of water to a boil and cook your eggs for 6 minutes. Remove the eggs but keep the water boiling. When cool enough to handle, peel the eggs.

Heat a glug of oil in a pan over medium heat and add the curry paste. Cook for 2 minutes, then add the coconut milk, fish sauce, soy sauce, and sugar. Add 2 cups / 475ml of water and season to taste.

Cook the noodles in the boiling water according to the package instructions, adding the vegetables to the pan depending on their cooking time (they should cook for roughly the same time).

Divide the noodles and veg between two bowls. Pour in the coconut–curry mixture and top with a boiled egg each, cut in half. Top with the chopped green onions.

NOW!

ALL I WANT IS SOMETHING ...

NOTES
→   *If you're vegetarian, always check the ingredients on your curry paste to ensure that it doesn't contain fish sauce or shrimp paste.*

224

SOPHIE'S CHORIZO & CHICKPEA STEW

My friend Sophie KT once told me about her emergency meal and I could not stop thinking about it. Here is her iconic chorizo and chickpea stew, which takes only 15 minutes and has five main ingredients. It really couldn't be any simpler. I've even used it as inspo for my Chorizo & Pea Pozole (page 74), if you want to make something similar and have a little more time. So this is from her emergency kitchen to yours.

8 oz / 225g cured chorizo

4 cloves of garlic

1 x 14-oz / 400g can of chickpeas

1 tsp smoked paprika

1 tsp dried oregano

½ tsp salt

olive oil

Roughly chop the chorizo and garlic. Toss into a pan with a big glug of oil over high heat and sear for 5 minutes until the oil is red and the chorizo starts to crisp up. Add the chickpeas with their liquid along with 1¼ cups / 300ml of water, the paprika, and oregano.

Bring to a simmer and add the salt. You can smash some of the chickpeas against the side of the pan if you like to thicken the stew slightly.

Serve as is, or with some crusty bread.

NOTE

→   *Swap out any beans you have! Throw in some potatoes or other veggies if you have a little more time.*

ALL I WANT IS SOMETHING …

SPICY, GARLICKY SOY SAUCE PASTA

Spaghetti aglio e olio – it's been the go-to quick-fix meal for countless folks for decades. Legend has it that even Italians whip it up after a night out (and half drunk) because it's just that easy to throw together. The core of this pasta dish remains true to its roots, but we're spicing it up with a few Chinese ingredients. The real star here is the chili crisp, a pantry essential (or it should be). Feel free to choose your favorite brand and adjust the heat level to your liking by controlling the chili bits.

8 oz / 225g spaghetti

10 cloves of garlic, thinly sliced

2 Tbsp chili crisp oil, plus 1 Tbsp chili crisp bits

1 tsp grated fresh ginger

3 green onions, thinly sliced

2 to 3 Tbsp soy sauce

2 oz / 55g Parmesan, grated (about 1 cup), plus more for serving   ↪ veggie Parmesan or other hard cheese

a small handful of fresh cilantro, finely chopped

salt

Cook the spaghetti in lightly salted boiling water for about 10 minutes or until al dente.

Meanwhile, in a large pan, cook the garlic in the chili crisp oil over the lowest heat possible for 4 to 5 minutes until it's really soft.

Add the ginger, green onions, and chili crisp bits and continue cooking over low heat until the pasta is ready (about 5 minutes).

Transfer the cooked spaghetti to the chili-garlic mixture using tongs, ensuring you don't fully drain the pasta. Add ½ cup / 120ml of the pasta cooking water.

Increase the heat to medium and stir well until the pasta absorbs most of the water. If it looks too dry, add more water in small amounts until the pasta is well coated.

Add 2 Tbsp of the soy sauce and the Parmesan, taste, and add more soy sauce if needed.

Stir in the cilantro, grate on the extra Parmesan, and serve.

NOTE

→　For this dish, I keep the pasta water lightly salted to allow room for a generous splash of soy sauce and a generous sprinkle of Parmesan without turning it into a salty whirlwind. Try to use as little water as possible for cooking the pasta – this means the water will be extra starchy, resulting in a super-glossy sauce.

ALL I WANT IS SOMETHING …

CHEAT'S DORITOS CHILAQUILES

This is basically how to turn a bag of tortilla chips from the night before into a meal. It's inspired by a Mexican classic, traditionally made to use up old, stale tortilla chips, but in my experience it is fantastic with a bag of Doritos.

Ingredients	
1 large tomato, cored	
2 cloves of garlic, peeled	
1 chile, stemmed	↔ ½ tsp chili powder
½ tsp dried oregano	
1 bag of Doritos (1¾ oz / 50g)	↔ any other tortilla chips
2 Tbsp grated Cheddar cheese, plus more for serving	
1 egg	
1 Tbsp sour cream	↔ yogurt
hot sauce (I like El Yucateco or Cholula)	
vegetable oil	
salt	

Blitz up the tomato, garlic, chile, oregano, and ¼ tsp of salt in a blender.

Heat a glug of oil in a pan and cook the tomato mixture for 5 minutes over high heat until it starts to become a thick sauce. Season with a pinch of salt and add the Doritos and cheese. Mix well and cook for 1 minute so that the chips are coated with the sauce but still slightly crispy.

Transfer to a plate, then add a glug of oil to the same pan and fry the egg until crispy.

Top with the fried egg, more cheese, the sour cream, and some hot sauce.

NOTE

→ *Regular potato chips don't work here, they must be corn tortilla chips, but any brand will do! Please don't use salt and vinegar chips.*

ALL I WANT IS SOMETHING …

NOW!

CHEESY GOCHUJANG TORTELLINI

I think we can all agree that premade tortellini is the universal knight in shining armor for college students everywhere. They are sold in almost every corner store, and these little pasta pockets promise a satisfying meal in less than 10 minutes. Now imagine them flavored like Korean tteokbokki – a marvelous dish of chewy rice cakes in a spicy-sweet gochujang sauce. These rice cakes can be a bit hard to find, so this recipe lets you have all the fun of the flavors without driving for hours.

½ an onion, sliced

1 clove of garlic, grated

1 Tbsp gochujang

1 Tbsp soy sauce

1½ cups / 150g cheese tortellini

1 green onion, cut into 1-inch / 2.5cm pieces

vegetable oil

EXTRAS

1 Tbsp chili crisp

½ tsp sesame seeds

grated Cheddar cheese

In a skillet over medium heat cook the onion and garlic in a glug of oil for 2 minutes.

Whisk together the gochujang, soy sauce, and 1 cup / 240ml water. Add this to the skillet along with the tortellini and green onion. Bring to a simmer and cook for 6 to 7 minutes until the tortellini are soft and cooked through.

Top with the chili crisp, sesame seeds, and a scattering of grated Cheddar cheese.

NOTE

→ *I used cheese tortellini because gochujang and cheese are a fantastic combo, but play around with the other flavors you can find – just avoid things like pesto!*

NOW,

ALL I WANT IS SOMETHING . . .

SPICY TUNA RICE BOWL

All of us have a can of tuna lying around at the back of the cupboard, and paired with some hot rice it makes a pretty great meal in less than 10 minutes – it tastes kind of like a spicy tuna roll if you squint.

¾ cup / 115g cooked rice

1 x 5-oz / 140g can of tuna, drained

2 Tbsp mayonnaise

2 Tbsp sriracha   ↔ chili oil, or my fave, both!

1 Tbsp soy sauce

1 tsp fresh lime juice   ↔ rice vinegar

1 green onion, chopped

Heat the cooked rice in the microwave for 1 minute. Transfer it to a bowl.

Scoop out the tuna from the can and place on top of the rice.

Spoon over the mayo, sriracha, soy sauce, and lime juice.

Sprinkle with the green onion, mix together, and enjoy.

NOTES

→   *Use a package of microwavable rice in a pinch – it's an emergency after all.*

→   *Other topping ideas: fried egg, butter, sesame seeds, crispy onions, black vinegar.*

NOW!

ALL I WANT IS SOMETHING …

BURSTING CHERRY TOMATO & HARISSA PASTA

This pasta brings together fresh cherry tomatoes and the spicy richness of harissa, complemented by a luscious egg yolk. It's a speedy pasta dish that effortlessly satisfies all your cravings.

2 cups / 150g penne	
3 cloves of garlic, chopped	
1 cup / 160g cherry tomatoes, halved	
1 to 2 Tbsp harissa	← miso or anchovies
1 oz / 30g Parmesan cheese, grated (about ½ cup), plus more for serving	← veggie Parmesan or other hard cheese
1 egg yolk	← 3 Tbsp cream
olive oil	
salt and black pepper	

Cook the pasta in boiling salted water for 10 minutes or according to the package instructions until al dente, using less water than usual in order to make a starchier sauce.

Pour a large glug of oil into a pan and add the garlic, tomatoes, and harissa. Cook over high heat, smashing down the tomatoes until they are slightly blistered.

Drain the pasta, reserving the cooking water. Add the cooked pasta to the pan along with a ladle of the cooking water. Toss very well and add the Parmesan.

Turn off the heat and add the egg yolk, tossing well to create a glossy sauce.

Season generously with salt and pepper and serve with more grated Parmesan.

NOTES

→ When big tomatoes are your only option, grate them using a box grater, leaving the skin behind, and use the pulp for your sauce. You can even use half a can of diced tomatoes.

→ Try using sambal or Thai curry paste as a savory alternative to harissa.

→ If you have some fresh basil or parsley, that would be great for adding freshness!

ALL I WANT IS SOMETHING …

NOW!

TOMATO & PEANUT UDON

Udon are fantastic noodles for when you're in a rush because they cook so fast, and this thick, peanutty sauce is perfect with them. Inspired by one of my favorite national dishes, the Ghanaian groundnut soup, I've taken the flavors of spicy tomato and peanut, and it only takes a few more ingredients to make this taste great!

1 Tbsp tomato paste

1 Tbsp smooth peanut butter

1 tsp chili oil

¼ tsp salt

4 oz / 115g fresh udon noodles

1 green onion

a small handful of fresh cilantro

½ a lime

vegetable oil

Heat up a glug of oil in a small pan and fry the tomato paste for 3 minutes until the color darkens.

In a bowl, whisk the peanut butter with ¾ cup / 175ml of water. Add the peanut butter mixture to the pan along with the chili oil and salt and whisk together.

Add the noodles and cook without stirring for 5 minutes until the noodles loosen.

Meanwhile, chop the green onion and cilantro.

Once the noodles are cooked and the sauce is thick, transfer to a bowl and top with the green onions and cilantro and squeeze in the lime.

NOTE

→ Don't skip the lime – it's essential for cutting through all the richness of the peanut butter. Switch out for a lemon if you must!

WOW!

ALL I WANT IS SOMETHING …

238

MUM'S EMERGENCY 10-MINUTE DAL

This is my mum's original emergency recipe. Her friend was coming down with the flu and she was craving my mum's dal. My mum offered to make her some but her friend was convinced it would take too long so they placed a bet. And my mum made dal and rice from scratch in under 10 minutes. Believe me, I've put her to the test, timing her over and over!

1¼ cups / 250g split red lentils

1¼ cups / 300g canned diced tomatoes

3 inches / 7.5cm ginger

8 cloves of garlic, peeled

½ tsp cumin seeds

½ tsp ground turmeric

1 tsp ground cumin

1 tsp ground coriander

2 tsp chili powder

a small handful of fresh cilantro, chopped

3 green chiles

3 sprigs of curry leaves   ⁓ optional but highly recommended

vegetable oil

salt

Begin by putting the lentils into a large pan and rinsing them with hot tap water at least three times, or until the water runs almost clear. It's important that the water is warm; this helps the lentils cook faster. Drain the lentils, put them back into the pan, and add 3¼ cups / 770ml of warm water. Bring to a boil, then boil for 7 minutes over high heat.

While the lentils are cooking, use an immersion blender to blend the tomatoes, half of the ginger, and 4 cloves of the garlic.

Pour a good amount of oil into a large pan, place over medium heat, and add the cumin seeds. Wait for them to start sizzling and dancing around the pan, then carefully pour in the blended tomatoes. Add the turmeric, ground cumin, coriander, chili powder, and 1 tsp of salt and cook for at least 7 minutes or until the dal is fully cooked.

To check if the dal is ready, press a few of the lentils between your fingers to see if they are tender. Add the cooked dal with its liquid to the pan of curried tomatoes and mix well. If it's too thick, add enough water to reach your desired consistency.

Taste for seasoning and stir in three-quarters of the chopped cilantro.

Thinly slice the remaining 4 cloves of garlic, halve the chiles lengthwise, and cut the remaining ginger into matchsticks.

To make the tarka, heat 4 Tbsp of oil in a small pan and gently cook the garlic until it turns golden. Add the chiles and cook for 15 seconds, then add the curry leaves. Cook for about 10 seconds until they turn bright green then immediately pour this aromatic mix over the dal. Cover with a lid and let the flavors infuse until you're ready to eat.

Finish with the matchsticked ginger and the remaining chopped cilantro, and serve with fluffy basmati rice or homemade rotli (page 151).

NOTE

→ *Don't skip the tarka – this wonderfully aromatic and flavorful oil will make the dal into something really spectacular with almost no effort! It's a technique used in Indian cuisine, tempering herbs and spices to add layers of flavor to curries.*

NOW!

ALL I WANT IS SOMETHING …

INDEX

ACKNOWLEDGMENTS

When I first started writing *Craveable,* my first book and something I had never even dreamed of for myself, I was naive. I really had no idea what sort of whirlwind it takes. It taking a village is an understatement – it takes all those who have lived in the village beforehand, those who are just visiting, and those who will be there after.

I am filled with the most immense gratitude that everything in my life has allowed me to keep creating, and for everyone around me who believed that I could. Firstly, thank you to the powerhouse women on my team, Alice Russell, Molly Costello, Katie-Jane Arthur, Daisy Janes, and, formerly, Maya Luthra for all the endless guidance and compassion. I really can't thank you enough. Alice, thank you for sticking through all my outrageous ideas no matter what and gently pushing me to write this book when I didn't believe I could.

To all my team at Penguin, Michael Joseph, Dan Hurst, Aggie Russell, Louise Moore, Beatrix McIntyre, Mubarak Elmubarak, Ella Watkins, and Anjali Nathani, thank you for giving me the creative freedom to make every aspect of this book exactly how I envisioned it. Dan, I am so grateful for your countless notes, edits, and chats on all things food – your passion for this book is what has made it special.

Thank you to my insanely talented photographers, Liz and Max Haarala Hamilton, for making our shoot days endlessly fun and taking such stunning photos.

Hanna Miller, for cooking and styling everything in this book, I commend you so much for all of your hard work. All of the food looks so spectacular (but still beautifully messy). Thank you so much for going above and beyond.

Roya Fraser, thank you so much for sourcing all of the beautiful props and backgrounds. They all fit the chapters so perfectly and I really feel like each photograph is a scene you want to dive into.

To Chelsea Clarke and Yuriko, thank you so much for your incredible style selection. I still can't get over the incredible pieces I was able to wear and how well it brought all the moods together!

Thank you so much to everyone at Evi-O. Studio, especially Evi O. and Eloise Myatt, for the stunning design and vision of the book, perfectly balancing the fun and usability that I dreamt of.

I wouldn't be in the position I am without all the support from my MOB family, thank you so much to Ben Lebus and Sophie Wyburd for taking a chance on me.

Thank you to all my friends, who have been the taste testers and the biggest hype people I've had in my life. For all the meals we have enjoyed and cried over, here's to many more big fat silly dinner parties.

Sebastian Graus, I cannot thank you enough for holding my hand every single step of the way for this book. Your unbelievable advice and knowledge on all food, design, and creative direction was invaluable. You are literally a dream partner in every possible regard and I can't believe how lucky I am to have you.

The biggest thank you to my entire family, from my 40+ cousins in every corner of the world to my parents and brother. Taking an unconventional career path isn't always easy in an Asian household but I'm so grateful that my parents were insanely supportive throughout it all. Thank you to my mum for sourcing my first cooking equipment from garage sales, filling my moped with gas before I went to work (just so I could get that extra 30 minutes of sleep), and always making sure there was hot food on the table. Thank you to my dad for believing in my ability to make all the ridiculous cakes and encouraging me to just do what I enjoy. And, finally, to my brother and my biggest fan (aka @hiteshgetsbaked), thank you for always being the first person I can call for help and for forcing me to start taking photos of my food.

255

Ten Speed Press
An imprint of the Crown Publishing Group
A division of Penguin Random House LLC
tenspeed.com

Ten Speed Press and the Ten Speed Press colophon are
registered trademarks of Penguin Random House LLC.

Originally published in the United Kingdom by Penguin
Michael Joseph, an imprint of Penguin Random House
UK in 2024.

Typefaces: Sofia Mohr's Seriguela and Matthieu
Salvaggio's Surt

Library of Congress Control Number: 2024949741

Hardcover ISBN: 978-0-593-79992-5
Ebook ISBN: 978-0-593-79993-2

Acquiring editor: Claire Yee
Production editor: Natalie Blachere
Interior designer: Evi-O.Studio and Eloise Myatt
Production designers: Mara Gendell and Faith Hague
Production manager: Jane Chinn
Americanizer: Rebeccah Marsters
Proofreaders: Rachel Holzman and Miriam Taveras
Publicist: Felix Cruz | Marketer: Andrea Portanova

Manufactured in China

10 9 8 7 6 5 4 3 2 1

First US Edition